JAPANESE EDUCATION

JAPANESE EDUCATION
Made in the
U.S.A.

Nicholas J. Haiducek

FOREWORD BY
John W. Oller, Jr.

New York
Westport, Connecticut
London

Library of Congress Cataloging-in-Publication Data

Haiducek, Nicholas J.
    Japanese education : made in the U.S.A. / Nicholas J. Haiducek;
foreword by John W. Oller, Jr.
        p.   cm.
    Includes bibliographical references and index.
    ISBN 0–275–93899–9 (alk. paper)
    1. Education, Higher—Japan—American influences.   2. Education,
Higher—Japan—History—20th century.   3. Educational innovations—
Japan.   I. Title.
    LA1318.7.H26   1991
    378.52—dc20   90–23749

British Library Cataloguing in Publication Data is available.

Library of Congress Catalog Card Number: 90–23749
ISBN: 0–275–93899–9

First published in 1991

Praeger Publishers, One Madison Avenue, New York, NY   10010
An imprint of Greenwood Publishing Group, Inc.

Printed in the United States of America

The paper used in this book complies with the
Permanent Paper Standard issued by the National
Information Standards Organization (Z39.48–1984).

10 9 8 7 6 5 4 3 2 1

CONTENTS

TABLES AND FIGURES

FOREWORD

Among the great changes of the latter half of the twentieth century—the tearing down of the Berlin Wall; the redrawing of the world map, especially in the Middle East and Africa; wars and threats of war on almost every continent; earthquakes, famines, tsunamis, and AIDS—no change is more apparent to the American consumer than the economic ascendancy of postwar Japan. With a Toyota, Nissan, Honda, Subaru, Daihatsu, or some other Japanese-made vehicle in every other driveway—not to mention the Panasonics, Sonys, and so on in our living rooms—American children of the next generation are as apt to finish out the series "hotdogs, apple pie, and _____" with the name of a Japanese manufacturer.

In the meanwhile, Japan has increasingly adopted Western dress, knives and forks, MacDonald's, Kentucky Fried Chicken, and pizza, American-style. Japan has learned to play baseball and eat hamburgers. Disneyland has been brought to Tokyo.

However, there are a few elements missing in the Americanisms of modern-day Japan. For instance, the names of Chevrolet, Ford, and Chrysler remain relatively unknown to Japanese consumers. Zenith, Magnavox, and Curtis Mathis are not apt to be found there. Instead of buying American manufactured goods, Japan has bought, imitated, or otherwise acquired the means to produce them.

The movement has been ever upward toward the nerve centers of modern industrial, high-tech society. Japanese companies already excel in the production of manufactured goods as diverse as automobiles and VCRs. Daily, Japan is gaining ground in the manufacture of computers and their components. Japanese robotics press at the frontiers not only of manufacturing but also high-tech applications ranging from self-regulating mechanisms to research on the composition of human DNA. In all of this progress, in addition to intelligence, perseverance, diligence, frugality, national pride, and personal humility, the common denominator has been to emulate whatever works. American pragmatists would do well to study the Japanese formula for economic success—as American business already is doing, at least at a superficial level.

In all of their borrowing, imitating, and importing the Japanese have shunned the acquisition of hard goods in favor of the ephemeral, ineffable, and intangible. Instead of buying American TVs and movies, the Japanese have bought the conglomerates that produce them. Now a conglomerate is about as hard to put your finger on as any other modern abstraction. But Japan strives for still higher and less tangible assets. Perhaps the least concrete goal of all—the one that lies at the end of Japan's proverbial rainbow—is what Dr. Haiducek simply terms "creativity." Japan can borrow, copy, improve, and refine, but the element that seems to be missing is the capacity to innovate and come up with the ideas of the future.

Because in the postwar era America has been regarded, rightly or wrongly, as the great innovator, Japan has turned to the United States for access to this undefinable quality of human ingenuity—creativity itself. The best route to this goal, Japanese planners believe, will course through American-style higher education. And so it is that a vast educational experiment is underway. It is perhaps the most expensive in all history. Japan is importing American colleges and universities. This book is about that experiment. While there may not be any place to stamp the words, as Haiducek's provocative subtitle suggests, much of the higher education of present-day Japan could rightly be labeled: "Made in the U.S.A."

John W. Oller, Jr.

ACKNOWLEDGMENTS

In the twenty-first century, the success of a nation will be measured by its ability to educate its citizens. This book is a tribute to those who see the future in sharing knowledge.

Following is a partial list of organizations and individuals who contributed much to the publication of this work: Masayoshi ("Mike") Yamano, President, Tokyo American College; Dr. John Oller, Department of Linguistics, University of New Mexico; Dr. William F. Sharp, Dean, Temple University, Tokyo; Dr. Robert Orr, Temple University, Tokyo; the office of Dietman Susumo Nikaido and the office of Congressman Richard Gephardt; Mr. Yusuke Kataoka of The USA-Japan Committee for Promoting Trade Expansion; The U.S. Foundation for International Economic Policy, St. Louis, Missouri; Davis Barrager of Nexus Communications, Tokyo; the colleges and universities in the United States that replied to the questionnaire concerning programs in Japan; businessmen and politicians in Japan and the United States whose actions and foresight have contributed to this newest educational venture; Winona Kennedy and Edward Tennant, whose support and reading of the manuscript helped to make this book a reality.

JAPANESE EDUCATION

Chapter One

AN INTRODUCTION

Today Japan is, per capita, the United States's largest trading partner. During the last half of the 20th century, Japan emerged from the trauma of World War II, defeated and "faceless." In less than forty years the country has not only recovered but has become a world economic power disproportionate to its geographic size. With a landmass of 378,000 square kilometers or 146,000 square miles, Japan is slightly smaller than California. Proportionally, it is one twenty-fifth the size of the United States and one twenty-third the size of Brazil. Comparative economic figures show that Japan's share of the world gross national product (GNP) in 1980 was 10 percent as contrasted with 22 percent for the United States (see Table 1.1). Based on a comparison of landmass and world GNP shares, Japan is eleven times more productive than the United States.

EDUCATION AND JAPAN AS BORROWER

One of Japan's main strengths is its ability to borrow and adapt information, technology, and systems. The latest venture, the importing of American institutions of higher learning, is by no means haphazard or accidental. Three periods in Japanese history help to explain this new open-door policy: the first is the era of the formation of Japan as a nation and the period of borrowing from China, roughly A.D. 400–900; the second is the era of the Meiji restoration and the importation of the industrial revolution;

Table 1.1
Comparison of Shares of World GNP of Japan, the United States, and Other Countries for 1960, 1980, and 2000 (in percent).

Country	Percentage of World GNP Shares		
	1960	1980	2000
Japan	3	10	12
United States	33	22	20
EC and OECD[a] Countries	26	31	26
Industrialized Countries Total	**62**	**63**	**58**
NICs[b]	3	4	7
LDCs[c]	11	11	13
Developing Countries Total	**14**	**15**	**20**
USSR	15	13	12
Eastern Europe	4	5	5
China	5	4	5
Communist Bloc Total	**24**	**22**	**22**
World Total	**100**	**100**	**100**

[a]OECD = Organization for Economic Cooperation and Development.
[b]NICs = Newly industrializing countries: Hong Kong, Singapore, Taiwan, South Korea, Brazil, and Mexico.
[c]LDCs = Less developed countries.

Source: Keizai Koho Center 1968: 8.

the last, which is still ongoing, is the post–1964-Tokyo-Olympics period, during which Japan emerged as a world economic power.

By looking at the aforementioned periods of history as concerted efforts to accumulate information and technology, it will be possible to understand and evaluate this latest change from education isolationism to an open invitation for the establishment of American branch institutions in Japan, a new direction in Japanese higher education policy.

In 1985, Susumu Nikaido, senior adviser to the Liberal Democratic Party (LDP), Diet member, and heir apparent to the post of prime minister, headed a mission to Washington to meet with Congressman Richard Gephardt, a future presidential candidate in 1988. Out of this meeting came an organization named The U.S.A.-Japan Committee for Promoting Trade Expansion.

In 1986, to support The U.S.A.-Japan Committee, The Committee for Promoting Trade Expansion was set up by the Japanese private business sector. This non-profit organization is located in the International Lobby in Tokyo. The International Lobby actually houses several organizations, one of them being the U.S.A.-Japan Committee, but the committee itself is often called the International Lobby for the sake of convenience and in this work I will follow that precedent. Through The International Lobby, Japanese prefectural governments and local communities sent representatives to Washington, D.C., with the goal of attracting American universities to Japan for the purpose of setting up branch schools. To date, according to the list furnished by the lobby (see Appendix B), 151 American colleges and universities have expressed an interest in opening some form of institution in Japan.[1]

For more than ten years there has been widespread discontent with the university system in Japan. Among the problems that generate discontent are the entrance examinations, which are probably the most difficult in the world, the waning myth of lifetime employment, and an awareness that the lack of creativity and innovation in higher education has left Japan vulnerable. Acutely aware of these problems, the Economic Planning Agency published a book in 1985 titled *Japan in the Year 2000*. In this publication they listed three main areas to be addressed: an aging society, internationalization, and maintenance of economic vitality.

JAPAN'S EDUCATION SHIFTS COURSE

Traditionally in Japan, higher education has provided the way to the "good life." If a student passes the stringent entrance exam for acceptance into one of the prestigious universities, the student is virtually assured a good job with a good company and lifetime employment. Generally speaking, students are not required to study or attend classes; passing the entrance exam is sufficient. The college or university years are viewed as a time for sports and relaxation before going to work. The university is also a time when the friendships are formed that are the basis for the "old boy" system that is the foundation for many business transactions in Japan. *Mombusho* (the Ministry of Education) is the governing body that controls education in Japan, including colleges and universities. By setting the higher education admission quotas, *Mombusho* helps preserve the elitist nature of the Japanese higher education system.

There is, however, a growing dissatisfaction on the part of students and parents. The university entrance system requires twelve years of preparation and inordinate amounts of money for special schools and tutors. At the end of all this, if students do not pass the entrance exam for entry into one of the prestigious universities, they are usually excluded from top positions in business or government and are effectively limited to a secondary social status. The student's future literally depends on passing a single examination.

Another motivation for change comes from business, which is rapidly restructuring and can no longer afford the costly process of training each new employee. Because of world business competition and the lack of control over sources of many raw materials, including oil, iron ore, and timber, Japanese industry is being forced to change tactics. There is a shift under way from labor-intensive manufacturing, such as steel production and shipbuilding, to high-tech industries, such as the manufacture of microchips, fiber optics, genetic engineering, and the creation of new materials.

As a result, there is increasing pressure on higher education in Japan to provide more training in the fundamentals of these new technologies. Universities can no longer remain the "holding pens" from which government and corporate Japan come to select this year's new blood. Rapidly washing over the current economic, social, and political situation is the realization that although the education system produces good, literate, hardworking citizens, it stifles creativity and innovation. In today's marketplace, hard work, loyalty, and long hours are not enough. There must also be an ability to create. Consequently, the Japanese have come to the United States not to borrow technology, but to acquire the *means to create* technology.

The most startling feature of this proposed union is that for the most part, neither America nor American institutions of higher education understand what is being asked of them. The goals, aspirations, and expectations of the Japanese have little or nothing in common with those of American colleges and universities.

NOTE

1. Actually, there are 154 institutions on the list provided by the International Lobby, but two of the entries are duplicates and one is uninterpretable (see Appendix B).

Chapter Two

JAPAN: THE BEGINNING

The ancestors of the modern-day Japanese came riding out of the mists of prehistory. Related perhaps even to the Persians and Finns, they migrated from the plains of Central Asia, across Mongolia, and down through the Korean peninsula. Finally, they crossed over to the island today called Kyushu (earlier known as Tsukushi [Munro 1911]). By the fourth century A.D., they had formed the Yamato state on the island of Honshu. When the Yamato arrived, the four main islands that make up Japan: Kyushu, Shikoku, Honshu, and Hokkaido were already occupied by the Ainu Indians. Among the other peoples that predated the Yamato were the Kamaso, Jomon, and Yayoi (Munro 1911; Sansom 1978).

The Ainu were Neolithic, while the Yamato were well into the Iron Age and armed with metal weapons. It took the Yamato until the tenth century to push them to the northern confines of Honshu. Although the Ainu may not have contributed greatly to Japanese culture, they did leave their stamp in another way. Through intermingling, the Ainu, who according to Reischauer were probably proto-Caucasoid (1987: 11), provided the modern Japanese with hirsutism and Caucasoid features not found among other Mongoloid peoples.

The language spoken by the Yamato ancestors was probably related to the Ural group of Altaic languages such as Turkish, Tartar, and Urgo-Finnic (Miller 1971: 14–26). Today, due to

heavy borrowing from Chinese, the Japanese language has become an amalgamation that is unique to Japan.

CONTACT WITH CHINA

The first written record of Japanese official contact with China
is noted in A.D. 57 during the Han dynasty. Much of this contact
with China came originally through Korea. In A.D. 265, however,
the Wei dynasty fell. Influence over Korea was lost, and for more
than a century there are no records to validate official exchanges
between the two countries.

It was in the latter part of the third century that the Soga clan
began to consolidate power. By the fourth century, through
intrigue and assassination, they managed to establish the first
unified central power structure seen by the Yamato state. Soga no
Umako put his niece on the throne as Empress Suiko (593–628).
He then nominated as heir apparent and regent Prince Umayado,
known in Japanese history as Shotoku Taishi, Crown Prince
Shotoku.

Prince Shotoku was one of the most important figures in the
history of early Japan. The Japan Cultural Institute places his
birth in 574. He died in 622. In Japan he is called the father and
the inspirer of the nation. In 604 he published a set of seventeen
Articles of Instruction, sometimes called the Constitution of
Shotoku Taishi. Actually, it was not a constitution, but rather a
list of seventeen ethical precepts from Buddhist and Confucianist
teachings that were to be followed by officials (Saddler 1962: 41).
He is credited with being the original sponsor of Buddhism in
Japan and responsible for its acceptance as a "state religion." In
604, he also adopted the Chinese calendar. In 607, he sent the
first official ambassador to China. The embassy consisted of
scholars, artisans, men with knowledge of Chinese literature,
philosophy, and history, poets, and musicians. Some remained in
China for ten to twenty years. As these people returned, they
brought with them ideas and knowledge that changed the nature
of Japanese culture and society (Reischauer 1987: 19–21).

Whether it was Prince Shotoku, the first Japanese "Renaissance Man," or the "Machiavellian" Soga no Umako who conceived of this far-reaching plan of importing knowledge, culture, and skills en masse may never be known. Prince Shotoku, however, is given the credit.

Ono no Imoko headed the first embassy, but it was through the tutelage of Prince Shotoku that it began. During his tenure as crown prince, painting, sculpture, tile making, ceramics, metal casting, music, and calligraphy flourished. The exchange of ambassadors and trade missions continued until the year 847. These 240 years of borrowing encompassed most of the Tang dynasty (615–907), one of the most glorious periods in Chinese history. This dynasty is famed for its painting, poetry, architecture, walled cities, ceremonious manners, opulent life-styles, and efficient bureaucracy, as well as trade and commerce (Nourse 1940: 47–48). Japan imported Chinese culture, technology, and language just as deliberately as Western culture and technology were imported after the Meiji restoration.

BORROWING CHINA'S WRITING SYSTEM

The Yamato state had no writing system, so they borrowed the Chinese system of ideographs. As early as A.D. 400 there is evidence that there were numerous scholars who could read and write Chinese. The first known mention of the study of Chinese in Japan is A.D. 405 (Aston 1972: 6). With the official acceptance of Buddhism as a more or less state religion came a rapid increase in literacy.

One serious problem arose from the importation of Chinese ideographs as a writing system. Chinese is basically monosyllabic and is noninflected. Japanese, on the other hand, consists of fifty phonemes and a wide variety of grammatical structures such as endings, post positions, and particles totally unlike Chinese. There were no Chinese morphemes corresponding to many of these grammatical structures necessary in Japanese.

Chinese characters are called *kanji* (*han*, "Chinese" and *ji*, "letters"). For the most part, each ideograph represents a morpheme. For Sino-Japanese words, each morpheme is represented by a single *kanji*. This is a highly complex and cumbersome system. To read a newspaper today requires an understanding of about 2,000 *kanji*. Since Japanese is a highly inflected language and many of the morphemes needed for meaning and comprehension do not exist in Chinese, no *kanji* exist for them. The Japanese, seldom at a loss for adapting, developed a system of forty-eight ideographs called *kana* for transcribing morphemes not covered by *kanji* (*ka* is Chinese for "false," and *na* means "word" [*American Heritage Dictionary* 1985]).

Modern *kana* has two styles or types: *hirigana*, which is cursive, and *katakana*, which is more angular or blocklike. Each has forty-eight characters corresponding to the same forty-eight sounds. In the *hiragana* and *katakana* syllabary charts (see Figure 2.1) each box contains an ideograph whose sound is a combination of the consonant given in *romaji* (Roman letter) at the top with the *romaji* vowel given at the far right. The "K" column, for example, thus reads: *ka, ki, ku, ke, ko*. The Japanese single-vowel ideographs are listed in the column just to the left of the Roman vowels. Both of these syllabaries are used to write foreign words and sounds in Japanese. Chinese *kanji*, combined with *hiragana* or *katakana*, is used to write modern Japanese.

Kana, although not yet fully developed, was widely used by the end of the ninth century. One of the most important sources for viewing the change from *kanji* to the incorporation of *kana* is the "Man'yoshi," a private collection of more than 4,000 Japanese poems that was assembled some time soon after 760. Most of the poems date from between 645 and 760 (Miller 1967: 33).

There is no disagreement that the Japanese writing system is one of the most difficult in the world, not only to write, but also to interpret. The complex orthography has been and still is an impediment to Japan's economic, technical, and intellectual growth. Despite several serious and some not so serious attempts

Figure 2.1
The *Hiragana* (top) and *Katakana* (bottom) Syllabaries.

W	R	Y	M	P	B	H	N	D	T	Z	S	G	K		
わ	ら	や	ま	ぱ	ば	は	な	だ	た	ざ	さ	が	か	あ	A
(い)	り		み	ぴ	び	ひ	に	ぢ	ち	じ	し	ぎ	き	い	I
(う)	る	ゆ	む	ぷ	ぶ	ふ	ぬ	づ	つ	ず	す	ぐ	く	う	U
(え)	れ		め	ぺ	べ	へ	ね	で	て	ぜ	せ	げ	け	え	E
を(お)	ろ	よ	も	ぽ	ぼ	ほ	の	ど	と	ぞ	そ	ご	こ	お	O

W	R	Y	M	P	B	H	N	D	T	Z	S	G	K		
ワ	ラ	ヤ	マ	パ	バ	ハ	ナ	ダ	タ	ザ	サ	ガ	カ	ア	A
(ヰ)	リ		ミ	ピ	ビ	ヒ	ニ	ヂ	チ	ジ	シ	ギ	キ	イ	I
(ウ)	ル	ユ	ム	プ	ブ	フ	ヌ	ヅ	ツ	ズ	ス	グ	ク	ウ	U
(ヱ)	レ		メ	ペ	ベ	ヘ	ネ	デ	テ	ゼ	セ	ゲ	ケ	エ	E
ヲ	ロ	ヨ	モ	ポ	ボ	ホ	ノ	ド	ト	ゾ	ソ	ゴ	コ	オ	O

to convert the system to an alphabet, the Japanese have retained their unique writing system.

BORROWING RELIGION FROM CHINA

Until the introduction of Buddhism around 580, Japan had no official religion. The arrival of Buddhism by way of Korea had profound and far-reaching influences. By the time Buddhism reached Japan, it had been so thoroughly filtered through Chinese culture that its nature had become Chinese. Two facts are primarily responsible for its ready acceptance in Japan: First, Japan was on the threshold of actively searching out and borrowing new ideas and technology, primarily from China. Second,

Prince Shotoku encouraged its spread by providing an umbrella of state sponsorship. The fact that Shintoism was already in place as a "native religion" caused little or no intellectual conflict.

Shinto, "the way of the gods," was basically an animistic concept based on feelings. Any thing or place that inspired one with a sense of awe could possess a power, a *kami*. As Japan was an agrarian society, much of life and prosperity depended on the elements and the seasons, and so it follows that many of the Shinto rituals have to do with spring, fall, harvests, planting, and birthing. One of the prime tenets is purity, which includes ritual washing or cleansing. Shintoism, Buddhism, and Confucianism provide the basis for understanding the elusive underlying spiritualism of Japan. Buddhism not only became one of Japan's religions, but also brought with it a vast storehouse of learning. Through the monks and monasteries came literacy, learning, and an awareness of a larger world.

The last official embassy to China returned in 838 or 847, depending on the source (Reischauer 1987: 33 or Miller 1967: 36). The great Tang dynasty fell in 907. Japan then withdrew into virtual isolation. Japan had spent two and a half centuries acquiring governmental structures, a writing system, technology, religion, arts, and crafts. Now she began a period of incubation that lasted virtually undisturbed from the beginning of the tenth century until the Meiji restoration in 1868.

Chapter Three

THE MEIJI RESTORATION
AND THE
INDUSTRIAL REVOLUTION

Between the tenth century and 1868, Japan was essentially closed off from the rest of the world. Society became clearly defined into four classes: rulers, warriors, peasants, and merchants. During this era a national identity developed, as well as a sense of uniqueness. At first the isolation was unofficial, but early in the seventeenth century the first Tokugawa rulers adopted an official closed-door policy designed to isolate Japan from foreign influence. Meantime, Europeans, spurred on by the reports of Marco Polo in the thirteenth century and those of the first Portuguese visit in 1542, began to look at Japan as a source of commerce and a fertile ground for proselytizing.

In 1549, Saint Francis Xavier, the Portuguese Jesuit, arrived in Kyushu. With the arrival of the Portuguese came not only Christianity, but also firearms, including the cannon. In the years of early contact, Christian activities were accepted or at least tolerated. Shortly after his arrival in Kagoshima, Kyushu, Father Xavier wrote in a letter:

> The people we have met so far are the best who have yet been discovered, and it seems to me that we shall never find among heathens another race to equal the Japanese. They are people of very good manners, good in general, and not

malicious; they are men of honour to a marvel, and prize honour above all else in the world. (Boxer 1951: 37)[1]

The number of Japanese converts may have been as high as 300,000 out of a total population of 15–20 million people. The acceptance of Christianity was most widespread in Kyushu, mainly due to the conversion of several *daimyos* (feudal lords) in that region. Near the end of the sixteenth century, Spanish friars, primarily Franciscan and Dominican, arrived from Manila. They were viewed as intruders by the Jesuits.

The Dutch began trading with the Japanese in 1609, and the English followed in 1613. The religious bigotries brought by these Western nations poisoned trade relations. Because of these rivalries, the meddling in politics by the Jesuits and Franciscans, and the discovery of a Christian plot to overthrow the Tokugawa government, edicts were issued in 1612 and 1613 forbidding the practice of Christianity. In 1614, all foreign priests were ordered to Nagasaki to depart from Japan. By the middle of the seventeenth century, Christianity ceased to exist as a force in Japan.

JAPAN UNTO ITSELF

A decree was issued by the Tokugawa government in 1637 that no Japanese should leave the country under the penalty of death and that any returning to Japan would be executed. During this period only the Dutch were permitted to remain in Japan. They were relegated to the small island of Deshima in Nagasaki harbor and carefully watched. Thus Japan's only window to the outside world became the Dutch trading vessels and a limited number of Chinese merchants.

In 1600 the Tokugawa dynasty came to power. The Bakufu, as it was named, was the administrative arm of the shogunate. It controlled the daimyos, who in turn controlled specific regions of the country. The daimyos paid and received taxes calculated on rice production and paid in rice. The formation of the Bakufu and their control over the *samurai* (warrior aristocracy) finally brought an end to the continuous warfare that had plagued Japan for so many years.

From 1600 until 1800 there were no internal wars to speak of. The last samurai war was fought in 1877. It was led by Saigo Takamori of Satsuma. The Satsuma rebellion was fought over the abolishment of the samurai as a class. The samurai lost. By the sixteenth century, most of the samurai had moved out of the countryside and into the castle towns. By the 1800s the samurai were no longer the legendary battle-hardened fighters who had enabled the shoguns to gain and hold power.

The Tokugawa era created a truly national state in Japan. Its authority touched every part of the lives of the Japanese people. The government told them who they were, what to do, what to wear, and what to think. There was very little movement between classes during this period, which lasted for 200 years. People were urged to be the best of what they were, not the best that they could be. These two centuries of servility inured the Japanese people to docility, to obedience without question, and to their role as followers. The only permissible contact with the outside world remained in Nagasaki through the Dutch. However, there was a fairly lively illicit trade with China carried on up and down the southwest coast of Kyushu, particularly in the Satsuma region.

THE BIRTH OF INDUSTRIALIZATION

During the isolation of the Tokugawa reign, preindustrial Japan developed a strong internal commercial network. The institutions and attitudes that would facilitate Japan's importation of modern technology were in place. Building the factory system and creating a modern economy would be the next step. By the early 1800s this network had matured and waited only for some outside force to set in motion the leap to a modern economic system and modern methods of production.

The change from the Tokugawa Bakufu to the Meiji restoration was not as abrupt as it might first appear. Many social dislocations resulted from the economic changes taking place. People began moving from rural areas to the cities. A new group of political leaders began to emerge. They were dedicated to economic change and industrialization. On the other hand, there were the old, well-established merchant families, most of whom had gained their wealth from the rice trade and by lending money to samurai and government officials. This latter group managed, often indirectly, to exert a great deal of control over the ruling class.

The Bakufu had in the meantime become corrupt. Bribery and collusion were common, and the oppression of the lower classes was extreme. In the early 1800s, when there were famines and drought, little was done by the government to alleviate the problems faced by the peasants. "The Tokugawa Japanese," as Hall notes, "lived out his life with his head bowed to a higher authority" (1964: 27). The peasants and the samurai became steadily worse off while the merchants, brokers, and Bakufu officials became wealthier.

For a number of years the Americans had been whaling in the Bering Sea and near Japanese waters. In 1839, Britain and China were involved in the Opium War. British gunboats attacked Macao and various other Chinese ports. Word of these and other events was filtered through Nagasaki by Dutch and Chinese traders. The country was beginning to feel the pressure from the outside world, but the Bakufu was unable to decide how to deal with the problem.

Even before these incidents, however, numerous calls were made to the Bakufu to put its house in order and prepare for an invasion by the foreigners. The strongest and most numerous of these calls came from the Satsuma and Choshu regions of southwest Japan. Many of the samurai and daimyos felt that the best way to deal with the foreign menace was to acquire Western science, guns, and technology. As early as the 1830s, Tokugawa Nariaka of Satsuma was smelting temple bells to forge cannons. Shimazu Nariaka, daimyo of Satsuma from 1851 to 1858, had 1,200 technicians producing cannon and gun barrels from the blast furnace and smelter installed there in 1853 (Hall 1973: 53).

FIRST U.S. CONTACTS

On July 8, 1853, Commodore Perry sailed into Uraga at the mouth of Tokyo Bay with four warships. The largest, the *Mississippi*, carried sixteen guns. Perry was to deliver a letter from President Millard Fillmore requesting the opening of some ports for trade. The Japanese attempted to temporize, but Perry would not be put off and the letter was finally presented to the governor of Uraga. After sailing around Tokyo Bay for several days, the American ships departed on July 16 with a promise to return the following year for an answer.

In February of 1854 Perry returned with a squadron of ten ships. He sailed up the bay to Kanagawa—today part of Tokyo—and dropped anchor. A treaty was concluded and signed on March 31, 1854. The Bakufu conceded to the opening of two ports, Shimoda on the Izu peninsula and Hakodate in Hokkaido. The latter was for the provisioning and resupply of American whaling ships.[2] Within two years similar treaties were demanded by England, Russia, and Holland. The Bakufu, powerless to resist, signed the agreements.

Townsend Harris, the first American consul general, arrived in Japan in 1856. His mission was to negotiate a broad commercial treaty. After lengthy debate and much maneuvering, the accords that opened the port of Yokohama to trade in 1858 were signed. The European powers soon made similar treaties, and the door to Japan now stood wide open. Foreigners were allowed permanent residence, and foreign businesses began setting up shop from Kyushu to Hokkaido.

RESISTANCE TO WESTERN CONTACTS

The general sentiment throughout the country was one of outrage. The cry: "Expel the barbarians!" echoed across Japan. Various incidents occurred in which foreigners were killed and foreign ships fired upon. In one such incident, American and European ships were shelled. They returned fire and destroyed the land fort responsible for the attack. They also demanded an indemnity of $3 million. This event demonstrated to the Japanese people how powerless their government had become. The subsequent loss of confidence by the nation enabled the clans of Satsuma, Choshu, and Tosa to unite under the banner of the restoration of Japan's supreme power, the emperor.

The coup that brought about the Meiji restoration was relatively bloodless. The emperor Komei, who reigned from 1846, died of smallpox in February of 1867. His son, Prince Mutsuhito, was enthroned at the age of fifteen as the emperor Meiji. Within months, Shogun Keiki was persuaded to hand back his administrative powers to the emperor. The last shogun of Japan resigned on November 19, 1867.

Subsequently, the Imperial Oath, or Charter Oath, committed the new government to "seeking knowledge from all over the world." Its aim was to make Japan as rich and powerful as Western nations and to do this by borrowing their technology and reforming Japan's institutions along Western lines.[3] The new imperial government was a coalition of men mainly from Satsuma, Choshu, and Tosa who had long been anti-Bakufu. By 1869, enough stability had been achieved to issue an edict that all land registers, lands held by the daimyos, be returned to the emperor. The daimyos were, in most cases, appointed governors of their old domains.

In the first decade of the Meiji, change occurred at a dizzying rate. The first railroad, from rolling stock to rail spikes, was imported and set up between Tokyo and Yokohama in 1872. The judicial and penal codes were revised, a postal service established, the Gregorian calendar and seven-day week adopted, and silver coinage issued with the yen as the basic unit.

JAPAN FORMALIZES EDUCATION

In 1871 *Mombusho* (the Ministry of Education) was established, along with a plan for universal education. The early Meiji leaders understood the importance of education. Business and industry needed a body of people who possessed reading, writing, and math skills. The military needed men who understood or could be taught the basics of Western science and technology. For these political leaders, education was not meant to develop young minds but rather to develop a strong state. Education was a tool of the state to be used to turn out obedient, loyal, reliable subjects who could serve as the basis for the creation of a modern, powerful nation second to none.

Much of Japan's present-day academic system is owed to Mori Arinori (1847–1889). Mori was born in Kagoshima Prefecture in the Satsuma region of southwestern Japan. At the age of eighteen, despite the edict of death for anyone who traveled outside Japan, Mori, with four local government officials and thirteen other students, was sent to England to study Western academic, economic, and diplomatic systems.

Mori returned in 1868 and went to work in the Foreign Ministry, where his knowledge of the West, his linguistic skills, and his Satsuma connections were sorely needed. Three years later, he was sent to Washington, D.C., as the first Japanese diplomat to be stationed in the United States. He arrived in February of 1871, at the age of twenty-three. During his tenure as chargé d'affaires, he diligently investigated American educational institutions at all levels. In 1872, he proposed a joint venture between the United States and Japan to set up various schools in Japan, staffed by American teachers, with English as the language of instruction. Another, more radical proposal made was to change the national language of Japan to English. In order to facilitate the process, he suggested simplifying English spelling and eliminating most of the irregular verbs. Needless to say, some of his views were not well received in Japan.

Mori was also acutely aware of the need for technical, industrial, and commercial education in Japan. His inquiries in this area led as far west as the state of Illinois. On May 23, 1872, John Eaton, U.S. commissioner of education, sent a letter of introduction on behalf of Mori to Dr. J. M. Gregory, president of Illinois Industrial University, today the University of Illinois.

At that time, Dr. Gregory was one of America's leaders in the area of vocational and industrial education. Mori returned to Japan in July of 1873 (Hall 1973: 180).

In the first two decades of the Meiji period, a number of private universities were started in the Tokyo area. Hosei, Chuo, Keio, and Waseda all date back to this period. Tokyo Imperial University was the only state university at this time. Mori was appointed commissioner of the *Mombusho* in 1884 and minister of education in 1886. As minister of education, he promoted women's education and the separation of religion and education. He also encouraged the opening of technical and vocational institutions. He agreed with his peers that the purpose of education was service to the state. The prime goals were character building and the creation of patriotic and morally upright subjects, rather than the training of the mind or the acquisition of specific skills.

One unforeseen legacy that Mori left Japan's education system, one that still plagues it today, is a lack of spontaneity. The roots of this lie in one basic miscalculation. Since Mori believed strongly in physical fitness, in 1887 he introduced military-style drills, calisthenics, and discipline into the curriculum. Within a short time, these spilled over into the dormitory, the refectory, and even the classroom. From there, they spread to the teacher training institutes and thus became a self-perpetuating feature of Japanese education. Given the Japanese nature and culture, it is easy to understand how this happened, but obviously Mori never intended this to be the outcome of such a simple idea. Mori was assassinated on February 11, 1889, the day of the promulgation of Japan's first constitution.[4]

The Meiji era lasted forty-five years, from 1867 to 1912. During these years Japan was literally catapulted from a feudal society into a world power. The government sponsored many private enterprises, although it maintained control over public utilities, railways, the telegraph system, and other industries considered vital to the national interest. The government was involved in shipbuilding, mining, and the textile and silk industry. An entire state-of-the-art spinning mill was bought, shipped to

Japan, and reassembled there. Foreign technicians were brought in to teach the Japanese everything from managerial skills to maintenance.

In the 1870s agricultural experts were brought in from England and the United States. At one point, the government went so far as to sponsor "taxi dance halls" to promote Westernization. The new fads created many new kinds of jobs and manufacturing. Items such as clocks, umbrellas, Western-style clothes, cameras, cigars, and cigarettes were much in vogue. Printing presses came into use and created a whole new demand for newspapers, pamphlets, and magazines. This is not to say that all of Japan had undergone a complete change. In the early 1900s, 67 percent of the population was still involved in some sort of agricultural activity or fishing (Duus 1976: 145).

In February of 1889, the emperor gave the Japanese people their first constitution. It called for an elected national assembly, the Diet. The assembly was bicameral, with a house of popularly elected representatives and a house of peers that was in the hands of the hereditary aristocracy. It also had a cabinet and the post of prime minister. One unanticipated result of the new constitution, so praised by Western powers, was that it laid the groundwork for Japan's future militarism. The military was given a cabinet post, with a vote on the budget as well as the power to bring down the government. The constitution required that the military post be filled. If the war minister chose not to participate in the government, the cabinet fell. The military answered to no civilian control. They answered directly to the emperor.

In 1894, Japan went to war with China over the issue of control over Korea. The war was over by February 1895, and the Chinese were forced to pay a large indemnity. According to Saddler, "The Japanese Navy grew from 59,000 tons at the time of the Sino-Japanese War in 1894 to 770,000 tons in 1921" (1962: 259). By February of 1902, Japan was at war again, this time with Russia. Russian aggression and territorial expansion into Manchuria and Korea provoked the war. It ended in 1905 when the Japanese fleet, under Admiral Togō, destroyed the Russian fleet in the Sea of

Japan. Admiral Togō's flagship, *Mikasa*, was a light steam cruiser purchased from the British. President Theodore Roosevelt was the intermediary who brought the two nations to terms.

By now Japan had emerged as a world power. She had decisively defeated one of the strongest European powers. What startled the rest of the world was that only fifty years before, Commodore Perry had terrorized the entire nation of Japan with only four ships.

EDUCATION IN THE MEIJI MOLD

The years of the Meiji period were years spent primarily in borrowing, studying, and adapting Western ideas, technology, science, and institutions. Having been successful in two wars and having acquired colonies (Taiwan, Korea, and parts of Manchuria), Japan was following the lead of the Europeans.

Emperor Meiji died on July 30, 1912, and was succeeded by Emperor Taisho (1912–1926). World War I broke out in 1914. Japan, having signed the Anglo-Japanese Alliance pact in 1902, was on the side of the Allies. The war proved to be a tremendous economic boost for the Japanese economy. Japan supplied much needed textiles, steel, munitions, and other war matériel to the Europeans. Japanese businessmen also took advantage of the situation to enter markets formerly closed to them by Western monopolies. Japan went to the Versailles Peace Conference in 1919 as a world military and economic power and for the first time was officially recognized as one of the "Big Five."

The empire had expanded considerably, and Japan's dominance in Asia was confirmed. She had also become a creditor nation rather than a debtor nation. The *zaibatsu*—business conglomerates often supported by the government, such as Mitsui, Mitsubishi, and Sumitomo, already old and wealthy—became extremely rich during this period. The rise of the "salaryman" (white-collar worker), lifetime employment, and factories, which increased in number and size, provided the basis for a middle class. Even so, the rich got richer and the poor did not. The emphasis was on creating a strong, wealthy Japan, not a strong, wealthy population.

By the end of World War I, the small oligarchy that had created the Meiji restoration and had controlled Japan for fifty years had either died or retired. The *zaibatsu* often controlled the Diet, due to the unique government-business relationship that developed in the early days of Japan's industrialization. The normal form of government was based on coalitions. Cabinets were formed and dissolved in rapid succession. Political assassinations were all too frequent. Bribery was common and widespread. As a result, despite the economic progress, political instability riddled the Japanese government.

THE RETURN OF NATIONALISM

Since the 1880s, the military had pursued a policy of expansionism. This was often done behind the scenes, cloaked in the guise of "the wish of the emperor." In contrast, during the "roaring twenties" the "flapper" arrived in Tokyo and became *moga*, "modern girl," with her male counterpart being *mobo*, "modern boy" (Miller 1967: 249).

On September 1, 1923, a killer earthquake struck Tokyo, Yokohama, and the surrounding areas. The fire and destruction that ensued left more than 100,000 dead or missing and another 52,000 injured. The suffering, disease, and homelessness actually accelerated the social changes already in progress. Downtown Tokyo was rebuilt along Western styles, with wide boulevards and tall, reinforced concrete buildings of steel and glass. The "new look" proved to the Japanese that they were indeed a modern and civilized nation.

The American stock market crash of 1929 brought on a worldwide economic depression. Economic barriers were raised in countries around the world to protect domestic markets. Japan was hard hit, particularly in the areas of cotton and silk, which made up the bulk of her export economy. By 1930, many Japanese, including some of the *zaibatsu*, began to support the militarist idea of "imperial acquisition." Japan's vulnerability due to the lack of raw materials and lack of market control was evident throughout the country and on all levels. The military began deciding its own policy. It manufactured the "Manchurian Incident" of 1931 as an excuse for the army to take over all of Manchuria and set up a colony or puppet state, which it renamed Manchukuo.

The civilian government was showing signs of ultranationalism as well. The Peace Preservation Law was passed in 1925 by the Diet. It severely curtailed the right of free speech and political activities that might be harmful to the country. It gave even greater power to the police to eradicate what were termed "dangerous thoughts." Any thought that questioned the position of the emperor or challenged other basic political or economic beliefs of the ruling groups was considered dangerous (Reischauer 1987: 167). As the economic depression deepened, antiforeign sentiment grew and supernationalism began to replace democracy.

The Taisho period ended on Christmas Day, 1926. He was succeeded by his son, Hirohito (1901–1988), whose reign was given the name Showa (Radiant Peace). His tenure of sixty-two years was the longest in Japanese history. It also ushered in one of the most turbulent periods of the twentieth century.

The military budget, according to Duus, increased "from 450 million Yen in 1931 to 1.4 billion Yen in 1937" (1976: 219). Japan withdrew from the League of Nations in December of 1933. By 1937 Japan was again at war with China, and in 1938 the National Mobilization Act was issued. Gradually, the military gained control of the media. This began a vicious cycle of indoctrination that generated more acceptance of the actions taken by the military and the supernationalists.

Democracy died in 1940 when the political parties voted themselves out of existence and joined the Imperial Assistance Association. In that same year, the Tripartite Alliance pact was signed by Japan, Germany, and Italy. What followed was World War II.

NOTES

1. Boxer (1951) gives a complete study of Christianity in Japan during this period.

2. For a historical overview of Perry's voyage and American attitudes between 1849 and 1854, see Palmer 1857.

3. For a complete reading of the Imperial Oath, see Tsunoda, et al. 1958: 643–644.

4. For a deeper understanding of Mori Arinori and the period in which he worked, see Hall 1973.

Chapter Four

POST-TOKYO-OLYMPICS: JAPAN REBORN

When Japan finally surrendered, the economy was a shambles. More than 2,300,000 military were killed or wounded, and over 800,000 civilians were killed or injured in air raids. Approximately one-half of the urban housing, 40 percent of more than sixty cities and towns, was destroyed. Fully one-third of the population was homeless, and most were on starvation rations. Japan's industrial sector had been nearly wiped out. More than 9 million tons of merchant shipping had been sunk or destroyed.

Tokyo suffered more damage from bombing and incendiary firestorms than it had in the killer earthquake of 1923. On August 6, 1945, the first atomic bomb was dropped on Hiroshima. Three days later, a second was dropped on Nagasaki. The war, which had been irretrievably lost since 1943, was ended by Emperor Hirohito's radio address. On August 15, 1945, Japan began to "bear the unbearable and suffer the insufferable" (Saddler, 1962: 293). Japan was an occupied nation from 1945 to 1952. General MacArthur as Supreme Commander for the Allied Powers (SCAP) was in charge of the hundreds of civilian soldiers, lawyers, educators, technicians, and businessmen who were to re-create Japan.

A new constitution was written containing numerous changes in the political structure. Article IX abolished the problem of military control by forbidding Japan the possession of any armed forces. The judicial system and administrative structures were revised, setting up a Supreme Court. Land reform was begun in order to eliminate absentee landlords. The *zaibatsu* were dismantled, primarily through taxation. The education system was decentralized, and a junior-high-school level was added and made compulsory. The school system was also restructured to be coeducational.

The cabinet system, redesigned along the lines of the British Parliament, was responsible to the Diet. The premier was to be elected by a majority of the House of Representatives. The premier could be forced to resign by a vote of "no confidence." The House of Peers was replaced by a House of Counselors, to be popularly elected every six years. The House of Representatives was given the power to override decisions of the upper house by a two-thirds vote. The primary goals of the SCAP were to rehabilitate and revitalize Japan. The method: democracy and decentralization. On January 1, 1946, in his New Years edict the emperor declared: "I am not divine." He thus renounced any claim to divinity or semidivine status ("Emperor's Life," 1989: 4–5).

THE REHABILITATION OF JAPAN

Japan received $.5 billion a year in support from the United States during the years of occupation. From 1885 to 1940, Japan had an average annual growth of 3.1 percent. However, after the war her GNP had fallen in 1946 to only $1.3 billion (Reischauer 1987: 237). By 1950, it had risen to $10.9 billion. The invasion of South Korea by North Korea on June 2, 1952, proved to be an economic boost to Japan. Although the world response was termed a U.N. peacekeeping mission, the United States considered this conflict a war. The American attitude toward Japan changed rapidly. The final peace treaty with Japan was signed by forty-eight nations in September 1951 and ratified the following year. At the same conference, the Mutual Security Treaty between

Japan and the United States was signed. This pact placed Japan under the military protection of the United States.

From 1951 to 1953 the United States used its numerous military installations in Japan as a staging base for the Korean conflict. Within one year, from 1950 to 1951, the GNP grew from $10.9 billion to $15.1 billion (Reischauer 1987: 238). Between 1956 and 1960, it grew at an annual rate of 8.7 percent (see Table 4.1).

The nearly total destruction of the factories and manufacturing systems during World War II caused widespread economic dislocation. However, it did provide the system with a direct benefit. Much of the prewar machinery and technology dated back to the turn of the century or earlier. During the postwar period Japan rebuilt with state-of-the-art equipment. Most of this was acquired by Japanese businesses through licensing arrangements with other countries, particularly the United States. The savings in capital outlay for research and development costs were tremendous. As in the Meiji period of industrial and technological borrowing, the Japanese adopted and adapted whole new concepts. In the process they often improved on design and technique.

Another benefit from the alliance with the United Sates was the reduction of the military budget. In 1938 the military consumed 16 percent of the GNP. From 1946 to 1952, 0 percent was spent on national defense. It was not until 1952 that the National Security Force was set up. Its budget was to be limited to 1 percent of the GNP. During the first few years after the war, from 1946 to 1948, there was a "baby boom," but by 1950 the birth rate stabilized, and it remained stable until 1974, when it began to decline. World trade increased substantially from 1950 onward. New and open markets for Japan's growing industrial products became available.

Between 1946 and 1960 Japan suffered a poor reputation for shoddy, cheap imitation products. At one point a town in Fukuoka Prefecture on northeastern Kyushu changed its name to USA. This spawned a widespread business in stamping products with the label "Made in USA."

Table 4.1
Japan's Economic Projections from 1956 to 1990 and Actual Results.

Period:	1956-1960	1958-1962	1961-1970	1964-1968	1967-1971
Cabinet:	*Hatoyama*	*Kishi*	*Ikeda*	*Sato*	*Sato*
GNP growth					
forecast:	*5.0%*	*6.5%*	*7.8%*	*8.1%*	*8.2%*
Actual:	**8.7%**	**9.9%**	**10.7%**	**10.6%**	**10.9%**

Period:	1970-1975	1973-1977	1976-1980	1979-1985	1983-1990
Cabinet:	*Sato*	*Tanaka*	*Miki*	*Ohira*	*Nakasone*
GNP growth					
forecast:	*10.6%*	*9.4%*	*6% +*	*5.7%*	*4%*
Actual:	**5.9%**	**4.2%**	**5.7%**	**4.2%**	**(5.3%)***

* Real economic growth figure for FY 1988 only (*Ministry of Foreign Affairs* 1990: 371).

Sources: Japan Economic Institute of America 1984: 13; and Keizai Koho Center
1986: 12.

Another factor that aided the expansion of the Japanese economy was the imposition of stringent import controls to protect domestic industries. By making low-cost credit available to certain industries and using tax incentives and stock purchases, the government was further able to stimulate the growth of new business.

From 1950 to the mid-1960s the production emphasis was on iron, steel, shipbuilding, truck manufacture, and other machinery. Japan rapidly became the world's largest producer of ships and the third-largest steel producer. From the early to mid-1960s, the production priorities turned to automobiles, motorcycles, petrochemicals, radios, televisions, computers, and related equipment (Woronoff 1986: 42).

By this time, Sony, Toshiba, and Hitachi had taken the advice of W. Edwards Demming, an American quality control expert.

Dr. Demming was sent to Japan after the war to help the Japanese create better products. The improvement in quality was so great that by the 1970s, numerous U.S. firms, such as Sears and Montgomery Ward, began to make Japanese products under license and put their own brand names on them. Between 1961 and 1970 the Japanese GNP grew 10.7 percent (see Table 4.1).

RETURN TO THE WORLD COMMUNITY

October 10, 1964, was the date on which Japan was reintegrated into the world community. On that day the Tokyo Olympics were launched, with tens of thousands of visitors and worldwide television coverage. The Japanese were able to show themselves and the rest of the world how far they had come since the dark days of the war. Japan had become a rehabilitated and economically sound ally of the free world. Expo '70, The Osaka Exhibition, which opened on March 14, 1970, demonstrated that Japan was the leading nation in Asia and could well become the leading economic power in the world.

By the mid-1960s, the United States was escalating its involvement in the quagmire of Vietnam. Japan prospered as a staging area and as provider and carrier of war matériel. The United States encouraged and sought to persuade the Japanese to become more involved, but this was at odds with a deep-seated pacifism engendered by World War II and the government's goals of a stronger and freer economy. Japan was still playing "catch-up" in technology and prosperity. The "export or die" mentality remained a driving force.

As a nation, Japan was vulnerable psychologically and economically. Its defeat and subsequent occupation left deep scars on the national psyche. Japan has often been called a nation of overachievers or a nation of workaholics. Much of this stems from the awareness of how resource-poor and vulnerable to the vicissitudes of the world market the country is.

In the 1970s, the precariousness of Japan's economic growth was emphasized by the "Nixon Shocks." In the summer of 1971, due to American business concerns over rising imports, the Nixon administration imposed a 10 percent surcharge on all imports. The dollar, which had been "fixed" on the international monetary exchange, was converted to a floating exchange rate. But even with the revaluation of the yen, the trade imbalance between Japan and the United States continued to grow. The last year in which the United States had a surplus trade balance with Japan was 1975.

The oil crises of 1973–1974 and 1979–1980, when the price of oil soared to $30–$32 a barrel, brought a rude reminder of how delicately balanced the "economic miracle" was. Japan is completely dependent on imports for its oil. Today, fully 50 percent of Japan's oil must pass through the Strait of Hormuz (see Figure 4.1). There is great insecurity in this source of supply. (JETRO 1988: 25). Japan is equally dependent on other imported products. Items imported in the largest amounts fall in the following order: oil, machinery, liquid gas, fish, shellfish, coal, lumber, organic chemicals, clothing, iron ore, meat, and textile products (Nippon Steel 1988: 133).

After having experienced the first and second oil shocks, the Japanese government adopted an energy policy aimed at eliminating the dependence on petroleum. In fiscal year 1986 Japan still had a high 56.8 percent dependence on petroleum as a source of energy. (The oil crises did have one benefit—they drove up the demand for small Japanese autos in the United States.)

The two oil crises did much to revamp Japan's economic planning. The high price of oil caused a worldwide recession. Japan's GNP remained at about 5 percent, but major manufacturing shifts were precipitated. Japan has all but conceded steel production and shipbuilding to the NICs (Newly Industrialized Countries). Fertilizer for export, textiles, paper, pulp, rubber, aluminum, and magnesium production have all been drastically scaled back and emphasis shifted to high tech. In almost all areas of manufacture Japan is in the process of changing direction. The Ministry for Economic Planning has also considered this problem and proposed some radical shifts in current policy:

Figure 4.1
Dependence of Japanese Energy Supplies on Passage through the Strait of Hormuz.

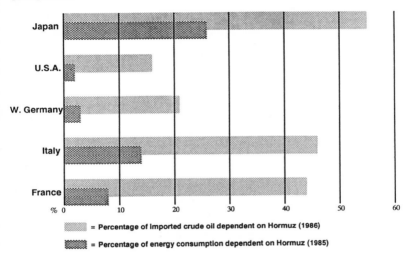

Source: JETRO 1988: 25.

Japan has achieved an economic advance without parallel in the world, now accounting for 10% of the world economy. Nonetheless, a series of changes in both internal and external conditions for Japan, as typified by a change in the international economic order with the United States as the core, limitations on natural resources and energy, and the progress of aging in society, is considered bound to have no small impact on the course of Japan's economic society in a long term perspective as well. (Economic Planning Agency 1985: 1)

First, there is no longer any room for the "catch up" type of thinking which seeks out models of industrial structure, technological innovation and national life in developed Western nations, and then positively introduces them into Japan to promote the progress of the nation.

Thus far, the history of Japan's development has been a history of adaptation to an economic society of the Western mold. Now that Japan has reached the economic level of developed nations and the social troubles of the West European countries are becoming clear, an economic society based on a Western framework can no longer be a model for Japan. From now on, Japan must open up a path of its own both economically and socially. (Economic Planning Agency 1985: 18)

This sentiment is echoed all over Japan. The plastics industry, for example, hard hit by the two oil crises and undercut by cheap imports, has been moving large amounts of capital into research and development of new organic substances and processes. Paint manufacturers are working on a method to use carbon fiber as a replacement for paint in the aeronautic, shipping, and automobile sectors. The textile industry, completely dependent on imported wool and cotton, has been priced out of the market by the NICs and has, consequently, turned to the development of new types of fibers for use in the medical and electronic fields. The paper and pulp industries have gone to computer paper and new types of cardboard. With an eye on a shrinking labor force, Japanese industry now leads the world in the employment, design, and export of robots and robotic technology.

CULTURAL DIFFERENCES: JAPAN AND THE UNITED STATES

Japan is rapidly becoming the world's most influential economic power. Compared with the United States as a nation, Japanese work habits, saving, investment patterns, and energy consumption differ considerably. Figure 4.2 provides a concise comparison of these U.S. and Japanese differences. Japanese investment in the United States comes to just under $34 billion,

Figure 4.2
Comparison of Japanese and American Economies.

COMPARING THE COMPETITION

Japanese direct investment in U.S., 1/88: $33.4 billion
U.S. direct investment in Japan: $ 14.3 billion

Japanese exports to the U.S., 1987: $83.6 billion
U.S. exports to Japan: $31.5 billion

Japanese imports of automobiles, 1987: 108,000
U.S. imports of automobiles: 4,589,000

Per capita GDP(adjusted). Japan, 1987: $13,000
Per capita GDP. U.S.: $18,000

Per capita GDP growth. Japan, 1960-87: 6.0% per year
Per capita GDP growth. U.S.: 2.0% per year

Japanese foreign-exchange holdings, 12/87: $75.7 billion
U.S. foreign-exchange holdings: $13.1 billion

BEHAVERS AND SAVERS

Japanese production workers' week, 1987: 43.2 hours
American work week 38.5 hours

Time lost to labor disputes. Japan, 1987: 256,000 man-days
Time lost to disputes. U.S.: 4,481,000 man-days

Unemployment rate. Japan, 1987: 2.8%
Unemployment rate. U.S.: 6.2%

Female share of Japanese work force, 1986: 39.8%
Female share of U.S. work force: 43.8%

Household-savings rate. Japan, 1987: 18.3%
Household-savings rate. U.S.: 6.3%

Industrial robots. Japan, 1986: 116,000
Industrial robots. U.S.: 25,000

Figure 4.2 (continued)

> ## CRAMPED CONSUMERS
>
> **Japanese pop. density, 1985: 3,900/habitable sq. mi.
> U.S. density: 130/habitable sq. mi..**
>
> **Living space per household. Japan, 1986: 874 sq. ft.
> Space per U.S. household, 1984: 1,456 sq. ft.**
>
> **Avg. rent 3-room Tokyo apt., 1987: $1,430/month
> Avg. rent New York apt: $1,150/month**
>
> **Food share of Japanese consumption, 1984: 19.9%
> Food share of U.S. consumption: 11.0%**
>
> **Per capita electricity use Japan, 1984: 5,418 kwh
> Per capita U.S. electricity use: 10,658 kwh**
>
> **Persons per passenger car Japan, 1985: 4.3
> Persons per passenger car U.S.: 1.9**

Source: *Newsweek*, February 27, pp. 21, 23, 25, ©1989, Newsweek, Inc. All
rights reserved. Reprinted by permission.

contrasted with less than $15 billion invested by the United States
in Japan. Japanese work a longer week (43.2 hours versus 38.5),
save more of their income (18.3 versus 6.3 percent), and in
general use their resources more efficiently.

Because of its size and population density, Japan has an urban
transportation problem of large proportions. Trains and subway
systems are some of the best in the world but are jam-packed
beyond reasonable capacity. The "magnet train," which levitates
magnetically above the rail, is one new design solution for more
speed and less noise pollution. Another solution being worked on
is a plan to locate subways underground at depths between 150
and 200 feet. Japan has also entered the space race. Refusing to
join with the United States for the sake of national pride, Japan
has decided to develop its own space program. A long-range plan
has been developed to provide a capability for space projects,
making Japan a serious competitor for the lucrative satellite-
launching business (see Table 4.2). Future high-tech activities
such as designing buildings for use on the moon and making

Table 4.2
Main Projects in Japan's Space Program.

Date		Name	Type
Feb.	1970	Osumi	Test satellite
Feb.	1971	Tansei	Test satellite
Sep.	1971	Shinsei	Scientific satellite
Aug.	1972	Denpa	Scientific satellite
Feb.	1974	Tansei-2	Test satellite
Feb.	1975	Taiyo	Scientific satellite
Sep.	1975	Kiku	Engineering test satellite
Feb.	1976	Ume	Ionosphere sounding satellite
Feb.	1977	Tansei-3	Test satellite
Feb.	1977	Kiku-2	Engineering test satellite
Jul.	1977	Himawari	Geostationary weather satellite
Dec.	1977	Sakura	Geostationary communications satellite
Feb.	1978	Kyokko	Scientific satellite
Feb.	1978	Ume-2	Ionosphere sounding satellite
Apr.	1978	Yuri	Geostationary broadcasting satellite
Sep.	1978	Jikiken	Scientific satellite
Feb.	1979	Ayame	Geostationary communications satellite
Feb.	1979	Hakucho	Scientific satellite
Feb.	1980	Tansei-4	Test satellite
Feb.	1980	Ayame-2	Geostationary communications satellite
Feb.	1981	Kiku-3	Engineering test satellite
Feb.	1981	Hinotori	Scientific satellite
Aug.	1981	Himawari-2	Geostationary weather satellite
Sep.	1982	Kiku-4	Engineering test satellite
Feb.	1983	Sakura-2a	Communications satellite
Feb.	1983	Tenma	Scientific satellite
Aug.	1983	Sakura-2b	Communications satellite
Jan.	1984	Yuri-2a	Broadcasting satellite
Feb.	1984	Ozora	Scientific satellite
Aug.	1984	Himawari-3	Geostationary weather satellite
Jan.	1985	Sakigake	Probe to observe Halley's Comet
Aug.	1985	Suisei	Same
Feb.	1986	Yuri-2b	Broadcasting satellite
Aug.	1986	Ajisai	Experimental geodetic survey satellite
Aug.	1986	Fuji	Amateur radio satellite
Feb.	1987	Ginga	X-ray astronomical satellite
Feb.	1987	Momo-1	Marine observation satellite

Source: Ministry of Foreign Affairs 1987: 203.

concrete with moon-based material also indicate that Japan is committed to a future role in space. It is entirely possible that Japan may even be the first country to put a man on Mars.

As of August 1986, Japan had launched 35 satellites. This figure compares with 22 for the European Space Agency, 20 for France, and 14 for Britain (see Table 4.3). The United States with 1,076 satellites and the Soviets with 2,204 were far in the lead. Japan, however, is engaged in an ambitious program for the future. Current plans project over $40 billion in spending, which will include construction of a space station, a manned platform, shuttles, and an orbital transfer vehicle (see Table 4.4).

In addition to the attention to space, much Japanese research and development is going on in pollution control, energy conservation, and energy-producing equipment. One example is the indirect involvement by the Japanese in the U.S. Mojave Desert project where windmills are being used to generate electricity on a large scale. According to NBC Nightly News (March 25, 1990), all of the generators on the windmills were manufactured by Mitsubishi because their generators "are more reliable, smaller, generate more power and cost less."

Experimentation is also under way in the fields of geothermal power, magnetic levitation for trains and vehicles, pollution-free ceramic gas-turbine engines, and new methods of treating and recycling sewage. Japan has already tapped approximately two-thirds of its capacity for conventional hydroelectric power generation and is currently experimenting with using ocean waves and currents for the generation of pollution-free electrical power.

Additional economic strategies being employed by Japan include overseas manufacturing and direct investment. At the urging of the United Auto Workers, local business leaders and American politicians, Japan has built a number of very efficient, highly productive auto plants in the United States. Doing this reduces the need for importing raw materials and avoids import quotas as well as a multitude of other problems. Another means of direct investment has been joint venture, or in some cases, the sole development of such projects as mines and timber harvesting

Table 4.3
**Number of Successfully Launched Satellites by Country as of August
1986.**

COUNTRY	Number of Satellites
Soviet Union	2,204
United States	1,076
Japan	36
European Space Agency	22
France	20
Britain	14

Source: Ministry of Foreign Affairs 1987: 203.

Table 4.4
Japan's Financial Commitment to the Space Program.

Development Cost in Billions	Yen	U.S. $
Japanese space station	1,060	7.07
Manned platform	480	3.2
Stationary platform	360	2.4
Orbital transfer vehicle	900	6.0
Orbital maneuvering vehicle	120	0.8
Shuttles	2,300	15.3
Co-orbit platform	480	3.2
Polar orbit platform	180	1.2
Space station program (& test module)	310	2.07

Source: Ministry of Foreign Affairs 1987: 272.

in Washington State, Maine, Canada, and underdeveloped countries such as Malaysia and Indonesia.

Appendix A gives a complete outline of the industrial restructuring currently in progress. It lists some startling changes from
converting small farms into food-processing operations and ex-
panding automobile-manufacturing expertise into space-industry
products, robots, and telecommunications. Companies previously engaged in iron and steel production are diversifying into
research and development of new materials, including heat-resis-
tant alloys for space and other applications. In addition, these
same industries are exploring new uses of metals in electronics.
Whole industries are phasing out some of their traditional activities and moving into entirely new areas. For example, cement-
manufacturing companies are moving into the fine ceramics and
real estate (see Appendix A under "Cement").

THE UNDERPINNINGS OF HIGHER
EDUCATION

Depending on the source, Japan's economic future is forecast
to be either "headed for disaster" or "well ahead of the developed
nations."[1] Whatever projection may be correct, the Japanese are
well aware that the key to the future is education. Japanese
education is considered by many to be the best in the world. Some
have even gone so far as to suggest transplanting various aspects
of the Japanese approach into the American education system
(White 1988). Japan has the highest literacy rate in the world,
hovering near 99 percent. However, the demand for excellence,
so prevalent from kindergarten through senior high school, stops
at the university doorstep.

As a result, if Japan is to succeed in its long-range commitment
to the ambitious restructuring of its manufacturing base it must
also change the nature of the higher education available to its
citizens. The current system is not providing the knowledge,
skills, and creativity needed. This, in part, explains Japan's
aggressive program to import American institutions of higher

education. It also portends a profound difference between Japanese and American educational expectations. While American educators are typically concerned about the near future, about issues that affect them personally and matters directly related to education, the Japanese are concerned with the broad economic and national implications of education not only for the present, but well into the foreseeable future.

NOTE

1. For opposing points of view on this issue, see Woronoff 1986 and Duke 1986.

Chapter Five

JAPANESE EXPECTATIONS IN THE CURRENT BORROWING EFFORT

How the Japanese perceive the need for the current borrowing effort is well documented. The new direction is spelled out in the context of Japanese expectations and goals with respect to the restructuring of higher education in Japan.

Much of Japanese industry, business, and government has been enthusiastic about restructuring higher education. Most of the resistance to change has come from *Mombusho*, the Ministry of Education, Science and Culture of Japan. This is not to say that *Mombusho* is in disagreement with the long-term goals of the broader society, but the ministry is powerful and, by nature, reactionary.[1] Through a variety of methods it controls what is taught and how it is taught. It dictates which textbooks are to be used, what and how future teachers will be taught, and what type of moral and social studies are to be included in the curriculum (*Mombusho* 1982).

In his policy speech on February 11, 1989, then prime minister Takeshita concluded that "promoting educational reform . . . and the individualization and revitalization of higher education is a major concern for all Japanese" (Takeshita 1989: 11).

THE NEED FOR CHANGE

In March of 1988, the *Japan Times* ran an article headlined "Japanese Universities Contemplate Reform," with a subheading: "Academic Institutions Feel Increasingly Limited by a Highly Rigid Structure" (Kirr, 1988). Michio Nagai, adviser to the United Nations University and former education minister, compared Japanese professors to medieval priests who forbade discussion to maintain the creed. According to the *Japan Times*, the "philosophy and establishment" is at work in Japan, molding and educating young minds in order to preserve the status quo (March 16, 1988, 7).

Approximately 75 percent of the research in Japan is done by corporate Japan. The shift from borrowed technology to high tech, future tech, and innovative tech creates a demand for an employee different from the traditional university graduate. New employees need more than good reading and math skills, dedication, and loyalty. Business economics has dictated that newly hired people have some in-depth background and understanding of the area in which they will be working.

In 1987, an assessment by a team of Americans and Japanese, referred to as the OERI Japan Study Team, published a work titled *Japanese Education Today*, in which they reached the following conclusions:

Implementing educational reform will not be easy. Ironically, this is partly due to the very success Japanese education has had in assisting the catch-up process. As in the case of people who come to a bad end precisely because they were once winners, so successful systems and policies tend to become inflexible and invite disaster by clinging to tried and true methods. Japanese education may be on the verge of this sort of "tragedy of the winner." . . .

Educators are inclined by nature to adopt a negative and passive stance on reform questions. The education system today, however, is suffering from a devastating blight whose symptoms are grueling exam score competition, juvenile delinquency, and violence in the schools. If the cause of this disease is the uniform modern school system itself, medicine targeted only at the symptoms will have little effect. The responsibility of educators is to diagnose the disease from a long term and comprehensive perspective and to implement a bold program of treatment.

How will Japanese culture, which has traditionally placed paramount importance on the individual's place within the organization, adapt to the coming "age of the intellect?" How can we achieve a balance among intellectual, moral, and physical education? How can we foster individuality and creativity while at the same time maintaining respect for harmony as part of our culture? These are among the questions that we must address as we face the monumental task of educational reform. (OERI Japan Study Team 1987: 66)

Two years earlier, the Economic Planning Agency not only reached the same conclusions as the OERI Japan Study Team members, but emphasized that "efforts must be made not only to develop both applied and improved technology, but also to develop individualistic and creative technology and train creative people" (Economic Planning Agency 1985: 63).

IMPLEMENTATION OF NEEDED CHANGE

One method of implementing the plan to borrow the apparatus needed to achieve creativity and innovation would be to follow the traditional pattern. From A.D. 400 to 900 Japan sent emissaries to China and through careful study and assimilation imported and adapted a writing system, religion, arts and crafts, and technology, as well as a bureaucratic governmental system. Later Japan followed the same pattern in importing the industrial revolution from Europe and the United States. In this current venture, there are echoes of the same methodology being used, first sending scholars, businesspeople, and scientists abroad to gather knowledge.

Support for this argument is found in the pattern of student visas issued to Japanese going to the United States between fiscal years 1985 and 1988. During that period the U.S. Embassy in Tokyo issued 102,965 student visas. In 1988 alone, 23,675 F category visas and 6,650 J category visas were issued.[2] Some of the J category students were high school students, but it is impossible to ascertain how many, because age categories were not available. However, the total number of all student visas issued in 1988 was 30,325. This does not take into account the number of Japanese students already in the United States who may have renewed their visas that year. For the years 1985 through 1987 the average was about 23,000 per year. A comparison of figures between 1988 and the average of the previous three years shows an increase of just over 31 percent (figures courtesy of the U.S. Embassy, Tokyo, March 1989).

After accumulating knowledge by sending people to schools abroad, the traditional method was to then integrate the new technology and information into Japanese society. The current venture, however, is more resourceful. The current procedure is to extend an invitation to the American colleges and universities to open branches in Japan. In order to speed up the acquisition process and to make it accessible to a greater number of people, Japan is bringing the source to the students.

Japanese companies are keenly aware that universities in Japan are not providing students with sufficient technical and linguistic skills necessary for the twenty-first century. An indication of this is that Japanese companies are not only advertising in Japan, but are coming to the United States to recruit American-educated Japanese students. IBM Japan, Sony, and Matsushita Electric, to name a few, already have active recruitment programs in the United States. (Iwaki 1988: 6–7). Hiring American university-trained students is becoming more necessary and acceptable as Japanese overseas activities increase.

INTERNATIONALIZATION AND
DECENTRALIZATION

Coupled with student, faculty, and parental dissatisfaction and the current needs of the business world are the stated objectives of the central government and those of the outlying regions. Former prime minister Takeshita declared as goals "the strengthening of international cultural exchange, the promotion of personal, intellectual, and other exchanges at the grassroots level, and the internationalization of local communities, including promoting international exchange at all levels" (Takeshita 1989: 11).

Internationalization is seen by many Japanese as the method by which they will be fully accepted by the rest of the world, particularly the Western world. One way to further this goal of internationalization is to have foreign education institutions open branches in Japan.

A second stated goal of the central government is decentralization. The Tokyo area is second only to Shanghai in population. As of 1985, Tokyo's population was rapidly approaching the 12 million mark, with a density of about 14,000 people per square kilometer (Teikoku 1987: 42). The strain on the ecology, utilities, public transportation, housing, and public services is tremendous. Another serious problem confronting Japan is that the nation is rapidly becoming an aging society, which will put even greater strain on the economic, medical, and human-service sectors. Former prime minister Takeshita's policy speech in 1989 underscored how aware the Japanese government is of the need for preparation and planning. "The advent of the aged society looms imminent," he noted, "and soon, one of every four Japanese will be 65 years of age or older, making it imperative that we adjust our employment, social security, and other economic and social systems commensurate to this new age" (Takeshita 1989: 11).

Figure 5.1 provides a graphic picture of Japan's aging dilemma. As the society is made up of an increasing number of older people,

Figure 5.1
Seventy-Year Graph of the Change in the Percentage of People in the Population Who Are Sixty-five Years Old or Older.

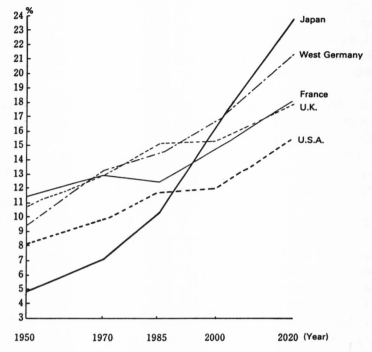

Source: Economic Planning Agency 1990: 300.

the viable work force is reduced and the burden upon the existing work force is thereby increased. At the same time, there will be fewer students in school and increasing demand on education to supply an ever more efficient and knowledgeable supply of workers. In the face of an aging society, with its declining productivity and a declining student enrollment, it will be increasingly difficult for Japan to maintain its economic vitality. Understanding these factors helps to explain Japan's current emphasis on internationalization and the radical restructuring of the manufacturing sector.

There is also the problem of decentralization. The overindustrialization and overcrowding of the Tokyo area demands that it be decentralized. Many of the prefectures, on the other hand, are underindustrialized and sparsely populated. Much of the economy in the outlying regions has been in an economic slump for several years. Yubari in Hokkaido Prefecture is a good example. The decline in the coal mining industry has reduced the population from 120,000 to 36,000. A new industry has to be found to support the local economy. They are actively seeking an educational institution willing to locate in Yubari. The local government hopes that the introduction of a higher education facility will lead to an influx of industrial capital (Kitazume 1987: 4). This would attain one of their goals: "the stimulation of the local economy." Other regional goals, such as "the enhancement of international understanding" and stopping the "Tokyo Drain" (young people leaving the local area for Tokyo), may also be served at the same time. All of these goals have received widespread support throughout Japan, although, as noted above, *Mombusho* remains lukewarm toward the idea of importing foreign institutions of higher learning into Japan.

JAPANESE GOALS AND EXPECTATIONS

Ostensibly, The USA-Japan Committee for Promoting Trade Expansion was formed in 1986 to reduce trade friction between Japan and the United States. That committee is still active today with some membership changes. Initially, some of the notables on the committee from the United States included Congressman Richard Gephardt as its chairman, Senator Albert Gore, Congressman Thomas S. Foley, Congressman Dan Rostenkowski, and Congressman Jim Wright. Some members from the Japanese side were the senior adviser to the LDP in Japan, Susumo Nikaido; Diet member Mutsuki Kato; Diet member Tsutomu Hata; and Diet member Kasuo Aichi, who is also chairman of the Standing

Committee on Education and director general of the LDP Research Bureau. Since The USA-Japan Committee for Promoting Trade Expansion was established, trade friction has increased. In 1990 Japan continues to sell America more than America sells Japan, and the U.S. budget deficit continues to grow.

In May 1986 The International Lobby was established, with offices in Akasaka in Tokyo. Its purpose is to support the Japanese branch of The USA-Japan Committee as the administrative arm for both Japanese business and government. Its current focus appears to be primarily that of coordinator for American institutions of higher education and prefectures or cities wishing to attract an American university to their area. The International Lobby has been assiduous in its duties of hosting politicians, academicians, and administrators around Japan. It has provided nationwide media coverage of these events.

The American counterpart of The International Lobby is a tax-exempt foundation, The U.S. Foundation for International Economic Policy, located in St. Louis, Missouri. The main document of interest from the American agency is "Draft Proposed Guidelines for the Evaluation of Branch Campuses of United States Universities in Japan" (November 28, 1989). This document and the Japanese equivalent are given in full in Appendices C and D. These two documents provided the basis for the research questionnaire and, consequently, will be treated in more detail later in this book.

Appendix B: "American Colleges and Universities Currently Interested in the Japan Branch Program" is a promotional list compiled by The International Lobby and is designed to encourage others to join in this undertaking. Questionnaires were mailed to each of the institutions listed in this directory. The replies were combined with other data to provide the research base discussed in detail in Chapter 7.

The reasons for turning to the United States in this venture are traditional and amicable. Japan has admired the United States and used it as a role model for many of its undertakings. U.S. higher education has traditionally been devoted to stimulating creativity, thinking, and innovation. Thus it is a natural source for Japan's latest borrowing endeavor.

> In order to maintain the affluent creativity of technical development and other areas, it is necessary for Japan to train those rich in creativity.

For this purpose, it has requested that measures be taken to renovate its educational system around the universities by strengthening internationalization and providing research incentives. In particular, in view of the changes in the population pattern, there will be an increasing need to enhance individual creativity. (Economic Planning Agency 1985: 156)

Throughout her long history, Japan has adopted and adapted myriads of ideas, systems, and technologies. This new venture to capture and inculcate qualities as nebulous as innovation, creativity, and inventiveness is perhaps the boldest and most innovative borrowing venture to date. The entire experiment from the point of view of the Japanese is part of an integrated whole. Japan's future is being studied and planned, and the current educational experiment is regarded by the Japanese as an integral part of that long-range plan for the future.

JAPAN'S PROBLEM-SOLVING MECHANISM

One of the most distinctive factors of Japanese culture, and one that is difficult for Westerners to comprehend, is the planning and speed with which "things" get accomplished. In reality, the mechanism by which change occurs in Japan can be painfully slow and at times frustrating. The process evolved through centuries of living in a space-conscious society. The lack of individual lebensraum dictated that some form of mutually acceptable guidelines be agreed upon. One of the precepts established was that the group takes precedence over the individual. Everyone in the group, however, has a right to be part of the decision-making process. It also requires that no step be left out or denied its own built-in time requirements.

The first step is the definition of the problem or problems. The definition is arrived at with input from all concerned parties. After this is accomplished, a cyclic process of reviewing and refining possible solutions takes place over and over again. The time factor is controlled by the problem and the mechanism. Once the process has been set in motion, externally imposed deadlines are of less importance than the internal clock.

Once there is a consensus on the best possible way of solving the defined problem, the group—in this case defined to extend even to the whole nation—pursues the same goals with the same expectations and in the same fashion. This sort of problem-solving mechanism functions well in a homogeneous society such as Japan. The process, in turn, reaffirms that homogeneity.

Often a dynamic result of launching the problem-solving mechanism is borrowing. In the case of education, more specifically the importation of higher education institutions from the United States, a need for creativity was defined by the awareness that Japan had, in many areas, reached or surpassed the level of other technologically advanced countries. What was needed, they determined, was the capacity to generate new technologies. Once the need became clear, the problem-solving mechanism identified the obstacle as the lack of creativity. The next step was to locate sources of creativity in action. The Japanese identified the United States as one source of this characteristic. They then narrowed their search to a readily accessible source: American higher education.

AMERICAN INDIVIDUALISM

Individualism is a principal element of American ingenuity. The historical demand for self-reliance forced the individual, often without or even in spite of the community, to come up with new ideas, to solve pressing problems, to be creative with the resources at hand. Traditionally, American universities and institutions of higher education have cultivated an atmosphere in which problem solving is expected from the individual student. In an analogous way, the institutions themselves function to some extent almost as individuals with their own special and unique identities, whether the institution be Stanford, MIT, Harvard, or Texas A&M. American colleges and universities tend to be "loners" and to compete with each other. The current export of branch institutions to Japan is no exception.

NOTES

1. For a study of Mombusho and one professor's description and documentation of problems therein, see Horio 1988.

2. Foreign students are issued one of two types of visas by the U.S. government. An F category visa is a regular student visa. A J category visa is for an exchange student.

Chapter Six

THE QUESTIONNAIRE AND ITS RATIONALE

With the formation of The USA-Japan Committee for Promoting Trade Expansion, Japan inaugurated the plan to import American institutions of higher education. Japanese expectations and goals, stated and implied, have been presented and detailed in the media and government publications and through The International Lobby. The American position, however, has not been as clearly delineated.

The American counterpart to The International Lobby, The U.S. Foundation for International Economic Policy, has circulated a document titled, "Draft Proposed Guidelines for the Evaluation of Branch Campuses of United States Universities in Japan" (November 28, 1989). For the complete document and the Japanese equivalent "A Proposal to Establish American Universities in Japan" (1987), see Appendices C and D. The "Draft Proposed Guidelines" consist of nineteen statements divided into five categories:

- AUTHORIZATION: Items 1–3 cover license, internal approval, and accreditation.

- SCOPE AND RESOURCES: Items 4–7 specify degree level, facilities, and language of instruction.

- JAPANESE AND U.S.   Items 8–12 cover recruitment criteria, aca-
  STUDENTS: demic credits, and where they will be recorded. It also requires the establishment of
  guidelines for the evaluation of the ESL program.

- CONTROL AND   Items 13–17 call for an agreement written in
  ADMINISTRATION: English, the designation of a single administrative unit for the program, and U.S. control
  over the academic program and funds designated for program delivery.

- ETHICS AND   Item 18 prohibits the selling or franchising of
  PUBLIC DISCLOSURE: the rights to the university's name for money.
  Item 19 requires that the U.S. university and
  its Japanese partner promote the branch campus program with factual, fair, and accurate
  public communications about the goals, objectives, academic programs, degree studies,
  and student services that are to be found on
  the branch campus.

The year 1986 saw the first euphoric headlines in Japan about the proposed influx of American institutions. By February of 1987 some serious negotiations were in progress. About this time there began to surface evidence of some severe problems on the horizon. Dr. John Young of Seton Hall University was quoted in the *Japan Times* as saying, "One of the major factors behind the U.S. universities' plan to expand into the Japanese higher education market . . . is the declining number of college-age youth in the United States after the baby-boom generation has passed college age" (Kitazume, 1987: 4).

This and similar comments by the groups flocking to Japan raised some serious questions. The news media, educators, and others began asking, "Do Americans really consider Japan a higher education market? If so, are they here only to line their pockets? The baby boom is over in the United States. Soon Japan is also going to see a decline in college-age students; what then? In the negotiations, Americans only seem to talk about how much money the project will bring in. They don't want to offer courses in science and technology. They talk about courses only in the humanities, because this fits American needs. What about our needs? If this type of education is to serve the needs of our students and those of the community, then we deserve answers."

The invitation to American colleges and universities to establish branches in Japan is based on clearly stated, albeit general, goals in "A Proposal to Establish American Universities in Japan." This proposal was a response to the pressure generated by business, the general public, and factions within the government who saw the need for the internationalization of Japan. American institutions, on the other hand, do not enjoy the same wide base of support for this venture. Perhaps the lack of support is due to the fact that most of the activity surrounding possible involvement is shrouded in secrecy and done with virtually no publicity or media coverage.

Furthermore, goals are often not precise and, when stated, have a tendency to be even more general or vague than those of the Japanese. In February of 1987, a delegation of thirty-five administrators, representing eighteen American institutions and four university consortia was on tour in Japan. Among those on the tour was Dr. Andrea King, chief legislative assistant to Representative Richard Gephardt. She is quoted as saying, "Part of our problem has been our lack of knowledge of the country, its history, its customs, its language, and, in particular, its people. . . . The Japanese do business with people they know. They are very reluctant to do business with strangers. The U.S. schools would counter that with a 50–50 mix of Japanese and American students, classes conducted in English, and internships for the Americans at Japanese businesses" (*Pacific Stars and Stripes*, February 20, 1987: 4).

All very true. However, the implications of the statement that "they are very reluctant to do business with strangers," belies the $49 billion trade deficit between Japan and the United States. Countering "with a 50–50 mix of Japanese and American students" may prove to be very difficult. Temple University, which began operations in Japan in 1982, currently has an enrollment of 1500, 78 percent of whom are Japanese. Life in Tokyo is prohibitively expensive, particularly if one is spending dollars.

In July of 1987, Gov. John Ashcroft of Missouri clarified the program goals in this manner: "The programs would help the citizens of the two countries understand each other's culture. Whenever we do business or have other contacts with Japan, we can do it in an intelligent way with an understanding of the social concepts that we are often insensitive to" (Todd 1987: 11). It must be assumed that when translated into Japanese these statements mean the same thing. With this kind of goal clarification coming from top officials of Congress, state government, and education, there is small wonder that some Japanese are asking, "Is this what Japan needs or wants?"

What are the goals of the American institutions of higher education that have expressed an interest in opening some form of program in Japan? Hundreds of administrators have made trips back and forth to Japan. Are American institutions of higher education well prepared to deal with Japan's latest borrowing venture? Do the institutions understand what is being sought? How well developed and planned are the programs?

The questionnaire was designed with these concerns in mind. Since all of the institutions involved are at varying stages of development from "opened last year" to "maybe in two years" and "we are opening in April," it was necessary to devise an instrument that covered the widest range of possibilities. Basically, it spans basic philosophical tenets to final planning and implementation.

Chapter Seven

THE PROGRAM: AN ANALYSIS

There are a number of sound, well-managed educational programs currently operating in Japan. Therefore, there exists a framework against which potential programs can be measured. Several of the institutions that responded to the questionnaire have indeed worked out viable agendas. Others may not have fared so well.

The program analysis in this chapter is based on data from a variety of sources: (1) conversations and interviews with educators, administrators, and politicians, both in Japan and in the United States; (2) newspapers, magazines, books, journals, and government documents from Japan and the United States; (3) responses to the questionnaire and the additional brochures that were sent; and finally, (4) personal experience in having been instrumental in the establishment of one of the first privately owned traditional American community colleges in Tokyo.

APPROVAL TO IMPLEMENT THE PROGRAM

Crucial to any project of this magnitude is doing the homework required to assure a sound base of operations. Often securing approval is more a political feat than an educational accomplishment. American institutions answer to a wide range of authorities, and these differ from state to state. They must also function under the jurisdiction of state laws and statutes and, in some cases, local laws and statutes. In addition, there is the regional accreditation association and the ever-present IRS to contend with. The IRS has become very busily involved with this venture because in many cases funding has come from the Japanese private sector and the institutions are being operated on a "for profit" basis. Regional accreditation associations are having a difficult time due to the fact that often there are no precedents for the types of programs and program controls being implemented.

Public and private institutions, two-year colleges, and community colleges all have differing structures. A two-year community college in Oregon must answer to the president, who answers to the local board, the local taxpayers in the district, and the state board of education. California, on the other hand, is more decentralized. The institution answers to the president, who answers to the local board and a comparatively nonrestrictive community college district office. Contacts with the state are funneled through the community college district office to the California State Board of Community Colleges.

Regardless of the structure, problems can arise. In Oregon, a two-year community college successfully negotiated an agreement with Japanese businessmen. They had the approval and support of the local board, the state board of education, and the legislature and had even taken the precaution of talking to the state attorney general. They hired a well-experienced individual from California to head the project and sent him to Japan. Before it had time to become well established, the undertaking showed signs of serious design faults, not the least of which was the criticism and hostility from the local taxpayers. They had not been sufficiently consulted or informed as to the nature of the undertaking, a costly oversight.

A California community college spent eight years of on-again, off-again negotiations with a Tokyo businessman. The project had the unqualified support of two successive presidents, the local board, and the district office, as well as numerous state legislators. The program was open less than two months before it was nearly shut down. The faculty senate felt that they had not been sufficiently represented, and they were furious. To make matters worse, some heads of departments had deliberately been excluded from the development process due to internecine feuds. When the time came to broaden the course offerings, based on increased enrollment and student needs, it was necessary to begin the in-house approval process all over again. Personal rivalries, power struggles, and lack of foresight all combined to jeopardize a viable enterprise.

An essential component of any planning activity is a checklist of any and all possible individuals and organizations having any influence on the establishment and operation of the program. Lines of authority and areas of responsibility need to be defined, drawn up, and agreed to by all parties. The basis for this diagram should be the position, not the person. People often change jobs.

One person, knowledgeable about Japan and based on the main campus, should be put in charge of the stateside operation. All contacts with the overseas branch need to be directed through this individual. Another consideration must be that, as students transfer from the Japan program to the main campus, it will be necessary to have one individual in charge of the process who is familiar with all facets of the system. This person thus becomes the resource person who can provide the essential counseling and direction needed to ensure a smooth transition between campuses.

ACCREDITATION

The Council on Post-Secondary Accreditation is currently working on new guidelines for accreditation procedures for overseas programs. There are a raft of problems facing the regional accreditation associations, including the lack of personnel knowledgeable about overseas programs, lack of uniform national standards, inconsistent guidelines, and arbitrary enforcement of standards. These pose some potential difficulties, so it would be wise to make contact with the association prior to signing commitments and beginning operations. It is helpful to identify someone within the organization who is sympathetic and empathetic to help in drawing up a working plan of action. These exchanges should be documented by memos or letters whenever possible. A few institutions have avoided problems with accreditation by not informing the regional association of their overseas activities. Unfortunately, the participants most likely to suffer from any problems resulting from this oversight are the students.

Because of the newness and financial nature of this venture, advertising for students is often necessary. Any advertising or written publication needs to be scrutinized carefully for statements regarding the earning of credits, transfer of credits, time elements for receiving degrees, and related concerns. Several lawsuits are now pending in Japanese courts as a result of allegedly misleading statements made to students regarding these issues. In a court of law a judgment depends not on what was meant or intended, but on what was objectively written. If there are doubts or questions as to the accuracy of a particular item, get a written opinion from the regional accreditation office.

THE OPERATING LICENSE

In Japan, all schools fall under the jurisdiction of *Mombusho*. The Ministry of Education issues all licenses. One of the most controversial issues involved in the opening of branch institutions in Japan is the refusal of *Mombusho* to recognize American colleges and universities as *daigaku*, or institutions of higher learning. As of this writing, foreign institutions are issued only one or two kinds of operating licenses: "miscellaneous school" or "language school." Many find this situation uncomfortable, and some even find it threatening. *Mombusho* sees its mission as that of protecting the moral and ethical precepts of "things Japanese," as well as ensuring that the students receive a proper foundation in the essential disciplines. The university system in Japan has evolved with a socially oriented dimension that supports the hierarchical nature of Japanese society. What is at stake in this controversy is *kao* (face).

In reality, however, this is a nonissue. Privately, officials of *Mombusho* admit that it is a little ridiculous to contend that schools such as Harvard, MIT, and UCLA are not legally considered universities under Japanese law. Accredited American institutions have nothing to fear. Corporate Japan is aware of this problem, but this does not deter them from seeking out and hiring graduates from non-Japanese institutions. Some traditions change slowly and need time to be appreciated before they can be fully accepted.

On the surface, *Mombusho* is at loggerheads with the *zaibatsu* and *keidanren* (industrial associations). Nevertheless, below the surface there is agreement. The overall goal of Japanese foreign and domestic policy is to create a strong, vigorous, self-sufficient economy and country. Everyone in Japan supports these objectives. It is inevitable that this "recognition" problem will be resolved and that foreign universities will be issued a special status that neither threatens Japanese institutions nor insults the foreign schools. In the meantime, either type of license, miscellaneous school or language school, will suffice. The only foolish course would be to provoke a confrontation over pride in the name of education.

LABELING THE INSTITUTION

Deciding if the program will be a branch of the main campus, a self-maintained autonomous unit, a joint venture (Japanese/U.S.), or some other type of organization will be dictated more by laws, attorneys, politics, financial arrangements, and other concerns than by design. Inherent in this decision is the further question: what degree of autonomy should the branch institution exercise? This is an issue that must be decided early in the planning. It is imperative to build a degree of independence into the chain of command and management chart. The on-site director must be allowed decision-making authority. If each decision must be cross-checked or, worse yet, made on the main campus, a major stumbling block has been created. Attempts at "home-based management" usually produce crisis management. Clear, open lines of communication between clearly defined areas of authority, along with a fax machine, will help create the foundation for a smooth-running operation.

ADMINISTRATIVE PERSONNEL

The question of administrative personnel is sufficiently important to warrant cautious deliberation. "Things" are done in Japan the Japanese way. This cannot be learned secondhand or from a book. It is learned by firsthand, on-site experience. There is little or no correlation between Japan and any other country regarding rituals of politeness, business traditions, and personal comportment. Intelligent, bilingual, administrative-level staff are a necessity to deal efficiently with the public and to provide accurate, effective translations of records and conversations.

The inclusion of Japanese personnel provides input, guidance, and insight into the decision-making process that would otherwise not be available. On the other hand, the exclusion of Japanese from administrative positions may well have a negative impact, since this can be viewed as indicative of prejudice or that the program is not truly committed to internationalization. Individuals who are completely competent and capable administrators in the United States may not necessarily be successful in Japan. Understanding, flexibility, adaptability, and cultural sensitivity are a few of the qualities that will enable the staff to function well in Japan. There is no substitute for "the Japanese experience."

TYPE OF PROGRAM: TRANSFER, DEGREE-GRANTING, ESL

According to brochures and other information provided by some of the institutions involved in this venture, most programs require students to go to the United States in order to complete their degree. This is an idea that seems to have evolved primarily from the desire to increase home campus enrollment. If this is to be a requirement, it should be based on a needs assessment or be in some way buttressed with a rationale. This requirement gives rise to several valid questions: Were the students offered an option? what about the student who, for financial or other reasons, is not able to go to the United States for two years? Have any provisions been made to cope with the "education limbo" created by this requirement? If one considers the high percentage of strictly transfer programs, another query certain to arise is: are the Americans unable or just unwilling to provide full education programs in Japan? One of the necessary program characteristics in "A Proposal to Establish American Universities in Japan" states: "The system of the universities is to be established according to the American educational system" (see Appendix D). The establishment of a "transfer only" type of program conjures up another quandary: American university students are not required to go to Japan for two years to complete a degree, even if the degree is in Japanese studies. Why is this a one-way street? The limited or qualified offering of degrees in Japan by American institutions may need further consideration if they are to provide the kinds of programs that Japanese have been led to envision.

THE NATURE OF THE ESL PROGRAM

No program in Japan, whether it is a transfer program, an A.A. program, or a Ph.D program, will be able to provide adequate instruction if the students are unable to comprehend the language of instruction. The results of TOEFL scores achieved by Japanese students can be very misleading and are not sufficient in and of themselves to be used as a placement device. There are times when a student may have a score in excess of 500 and still be unable to carry on a reasonable conversation or understand simple directions in English. Establishing a program in Japan places the institution in an "ESL situation." This is a circumstance in which all program activities are limited by the English language proficiency of the participants.

There are a number of ESL models available. Any model, however, that sets up "English as a Second Language" as a separate component will be ineffectual. Every class that a non-native speaker of English takes is, to some degree or other, an ESL class. The failure to integrate concepts and language-teaching methodology into all instructional classes from accounting to zoology is a disservice to the students and impedes the entire educational process. Each professor and staff member who is trained in ESL techniques will be much more effective in helping to achieve the overall program goals.

Individuals involved in this type of situation need to be aware of not only *what* they are saying, but *how* they are saying it. Integrative techniques such as requiring that term papers be assigned in each class and that these be coordinated with the ESL writing section help relate the language to all study areas. They also give the student an opportunity to discuss ideas and material not understood in the class. Such activities require the faculty to work together to provide cross-discipline solutions and cooperation. The traditional main campus egotism and rivalry between disciplines need to be taken into account when designing and implementing the ESL program.

Reading and writing are vital features of any language program. At times, however, they tend to overshadow other important elements. Classes in speech, drama, articulatory phonetics, and phonological reproduction need to be included in the curriculum. The less "foreign" a person sounds, the more effectively he or she can communicate with "native speakers." Some sounds in English do not exist in Japanese. The "l" and "r" are two renowned problems. If students are not taught how to distinguish between them and how to reproduce them correctly, their misuse will surface in writing as well as in comprehension.

At one point during the occupation, it was rumored that General MacArthur would run for president of the United States. When a local village heard that the great general, who was highly regarded by the Japanese, was coming to visit, they constructed a huge, elaborate sign saying: "Welcome General MacArthur. We Play For Your Erection." Phonemes do make a difference.

Teaching English as a Second Language is of necessity the cornerstone of the academic program.

RESOURCES AND TEXTBOOKS

The acquisition of textbooks can become a financial as well as a philosophical issue. One of the primary resources available in Japan for procuring textbooks is the representatives of the various publishing houses in Japan. Prentice-Hall, Harper and Row, and Newbury House, among others, are all in the Tokyo phone directory. These representatives travel the length and breadth of Japan and are storehouses of valuable information.

In one instance, the main campus had selected a specific textbook series for the ESL program. Checking with the publisher's agent revealed that this was a series widely used by many language institutes and *juku* (private, after-hours prep schools). If the students coming to the university were required to use the same textbook that they were currently using in *juku* or language school, the impression would be conveyed that the American university was nothing more than a glorified language institute.

At times the representatives can save the program money. If orders are placed early enough, they can be added to the company's bulk shipments. The agents do not sell books. This is handled through the complex Japanese distribution system. Consequently, their service and advice are not influenced by a sales quota. Getting to know these representatives will provide an invaluable source of information and help for any program.

Considering the ESL nature of all of the program's classes, careful attention must be paid to the selection of textbooks in all disciplines. At times a book is selected simply because it was written by the department chairperson. Overriding such a selection criterion should be the primary concern: readability. Convoluted sentences and unnecessary jargon do not promote learning under any circumstance. Likewise, social and political issues are often used in language texts as a way to teach culture as well as language. Too often the student has no basis for relating to the material and becomes confused and frustrated. Content must be appropriate for the teaching goals. One approach that can be of merit is to have a textbook committee. If clearly stated guidelines are formulated and utilized by a knowledgeable group, the results can be beneficial for the students, faculty, and program as a whole. Selection by individual faculty or department heads usually produces random results, which in turn affect program effectiveness.

Even though the branch happens to be an American institution and classes are taught entirely in English, the majority of students are Japanese. When they leave the campus, they are in Japan, with a linguistic and cultural milieu that is Japanese. There are few outside influences to help reinforce the classroom experience. Student textbooks are often the only outside link to the classroom.

The following is a quote from a required supplemental text for an Economics 101, Introduction to Economics, class:

Life-cycle Hypothesis. The hypothesis is that individuals consume a constant proportion of the present value of their lifetime income each period. Precisely what this proportion will be depends on each consumer's tastes and preferences, but provided the distribution of the population by age and income is relatively constant these individual consumption functions can be aggregated to produce a stable aggregate consumption function. (*Macmillan Dictionary of Modern Economics 1985: 243*)

An American freshman would have a difficult time understanding these two sentences, even diagrammed. This citation is a good example of nonreadability produced by jargon and convoluted grammatical structures. The textbook was selected by a newly arrived professor of economics who "had good results with it in his classes in the States."

THE ACADEMIC YEAR

In Japan the school year is divided into two semesters: April to September and October to March. Most students have made up their minds about which school they want to attend by January or no later than February. If the home campus is on the trimester or quarter system, any number of problems will arise in the recruitment of students, record keeping, and the transfer of students and faculty between institutions. The complications that the academic year can create are not limited to adjustments between two different school calendars. There are twelve legal holidays in Japan, in addition to other special occasions such as Golden Week, Obon, and Cherry Blossom Viewing, which are quite important in Japan. These may require further adjustments to the calendar. Needless to say, Christmas, Thanksgiving, and Easter are generally not celebrated in Japan.

Conflict generally arises between the main campus and the Japanese program over reporting methods. The main campus has a computer program designed to process specific information on certain dates. The Japanese program invariably requires a different set of data and different dates for its operations. The main campus data center is usually upset when someone does not comply with their requirements.

These reporting systems are usually designed to suit the needs of the university employees rather than those of the students. Hence they are generally inflexible. This problem needs to be dealt with early in the planning phase and not as an afterthought once the project is under way. On the surface, reporting requirements may seem a relatively minor concern, but in one case they quickly escalated into a standoff where the reporting center refused to issue grades and related information. This type of predicament generates a loss of confidence in the school, internal bickering, and, upon occasion, student lawsuits.

FOR WHOM IS THE PROGRAM INTENDED?

Based on available information, the majority of students enrolling in these programs are anticipated to be Japanese and Americans. However, as the *Japan Times* reports, "As of May 1, 1988, there were 25,643 foreign students in Japan, a 15.7% increase from the previous year. Among them, 88.9% were Asian students and only 13% of them were receiving scholarships from the Japanese government. The rest were either getting money from their home country or working part-time to pay for tuition and other living expenses" (Fukami, February 26, 1989).

Some students from the underdeveloped countries have come to Japan for the work but need a cover institution to provide legitimacy for student visa renewal. Recent scandals involving trade and language schools, where students paid tuition but did not attend class, have caused a crackdown by immigration authorities. The registrar of each institution should make contact with immigration officials to ensure that the school has the information required to understand and follow the rules and regulations regarding student visas. A strict attendance policy, firm enforcement, and accurate attendance records will earn the respect of the students and the community. It will also forestall unwanted visits from immigration authorities, as well as undesirable publicity.

Since the majority of students will be Japanese, the registrar or person in charge of enrollment will need assistance in translating and evaluating student records. Currently there are no concrete rules governing "credit acceptability." As in all systems, there is a wide disparity among Japanese schools, and what is an A in one may well be a B or C in another. However, since most American colleges and universities operate on an "open admissions policy," the major factors to be dealt with will be adequate placement strategies and a well-planned, well-executed ESL program.

The registrar may also be the person who should be delegated goodwill ambassador, responsible for paying the mandatory courtesy calls to all of the high schools and other institutions in the region. The local high schools will be the source of future students as well as a reservoir of information and assistance. Small things like this are critically important in Japan. A good neighbor policy needs to be established at the very outset.

LOCATION

Many cities and prefectures are offering very generous incentives to attract American institutions to their regions. Even though their motives are often not based on educational excellence, they are clearly stated. They hope to revitalize the local economy, stop the Tokyo drain, and attract business and industry to their locales. Former prime minister Takeshita and numerous high government officials see the need to "escape the over-concentration in and over-dependence on Tokyo" (Takeshita 1989: 11). They are promoting, in a word, decentralization.

The establishment of branch institutions in the outlying areas serves a number of goals on many levels, and the Japanese are wiling to pay a high price to meet these goals. The average sum for first-year start-up costs exceeds $4 million. In addition, the Japanese also offer free land or low-priced, long-term lease arrangements for facilities. Unfortunately, some of the American participants have not taken the time to do a feasibility study. Several questions that need to be answered are: How many students will be available? What are the needs and wants of these students and their parents? How can students from other areas be attracted? Does the home campus have the resources and ability to meet these needs? Free land and facilities and financial assistance are attractive, but of themselves do not provide a valid rationale for the creation of a college or university.

LOGISTICS

Demographics for the proposed branches reveal that several of the planned goals of the Japanese are being met. The fact that only two or three of the institutions will be located in Tokyo or in the greater Tokyo area is a boost to the idea of decentralization. The majority are or will be dispersed throughout Japan from Akita Prefecture, in the far northeast of Honshu, to Hiroshima Prefecture, in the south. A variety of problems, however, are beginning to surface in these outlying areas. At times, the recruiting of instructors is difficult. Or there may not be a sufficient student-age population to support the program. In some cases, several institutions are vying for the same group of potential students. Such seemingly small things as classroom and office supplies are often difficult to locate and slow to arrive. The list could go on.

The main reason so many students leave these outlying areas is boredom. There is nothing to do, nothing to keep students interested or stimulated. In order to survive, the institution must provide a campus life-style sufficiently exciting to attract and keep students and faculty. An indoor/outdoor sports complex of sufficient size to accommodate volleyball, tennis, swimming, baseball, basketball, and billiards needs to be included in the facility planning. Golf is the single biggest passion in Japan. In Tokyo people practice on rooftops, in the alleyways, and in their apartments, anywhere there is enough room to swing a golf club. Land is at an extreme premium in Japan, but if there is the remotest possibility of creating one, a golf course would be a major attraction.

Movies, theater productions, in short, an exceptionally attractive extracurricular program, needs to be developed not only for the students, but for everyone involved with the institution. Suggestions for activities should be elicited from the students, faculty, staff, and surrounding populace. As often and as much as possible, the local residents should be included in school activities. Regardless of the goals, making the institution a regional cultural center will ensure the long-term survival of the school.

RECRUITMENT OF FACULTY AND STAFF

Many of the participating institutions have indicated that the main source of faculty and teaching staff would be the main campus. At first glance this seems to be an ideal source. The big loser, however, may well be program continuity. Since many of the transferees would be in Japan for only one semester or only a summer session, more time, money, and effort would have to be spent on transportation, acculturation, orientation to the program, and additional paperwork rather than on the education process itself. Some colleges and universities actually plan to use part of their programs in Japan as a "perk for faculty members. High salaries and light class loads are being offered to faculty who would normally be unemployed during the summer. They are also using one-year positions for faculty who are no longer needed on the main campus because of declining enrollment or other factors. These positions are being tendered as rewards since "*they* [the Japanese] are picking up the tab."

Constant replacement of faculty members calls for constant training and orientation. It becomes expensive and inefficient for the system and has, to varying degrees, a demoralizing effect on students, since Japanese students often form strong loyalties to instructors.

Personnel orientation must also be a primary component of recruitment efforts. Not everyone can function well in Japan. It is an alien culture and difficult for many to understand. There is little that can be said or done to prepare the uninitiated for the cost and size of living accommodations. Consequently, total honesty must be a part of the orientation procedure. One of the goals of main-campus recruitment must be to secure long-term support and commitment for the program even after the faculty rotates back to the United States. Long-term commitment and low faculty turnover will enable a program to develop and expand at a reasonably steady pace.

There is a sizable cadre of well-credentialed, well-acculturated American instructors currently living in Japan. Most of them have taught English as a Second Language, regardless of their major field of expertise. Their experience can provide an invaluable and stabilizing addition to any American institution in Japan. JALT, the Japanese Association of Language Teachers, is another good source of information about potential instructors. Also, advertisements in the Tokyo papers, particularly the *Japan Times*, usually produce results if the salary and conditions are attractive.

STUDENT RECRUITMENT

The recruitment of students depends in part on the creation of a program image. Even though advertising has created problems for some institutions, the fault lies not in the advertising itself, but in the lack of forethought, planning, and careful proofreading of materials. Since these programs are a new experience for the Japanese public, it is necessary to convince them that attending an American institution is a desirable activity and that doing so will be to their benefit.

For this reason it is also necessary to create an image for the institution. Publicity is essential. The easiest and safest approach to promotion is through an advertising agency. This approach will also achieve the best results. When, where, and how much to advertise will depend on the size of the area from which student enrollment will be drawn. Advertising in Japan is highly controlled by a few large agencies, which in turn sell space or time to other, smaller agencies. Unknown or unconnected individuals will have a difficult time. The American Chamber of Commerce and the International Chamber of Commerce are listed in the *Tokyo City Source English Telephone Directory*. They are reliable and knowledgeable organizations that will be able to recommend reputable advertising agencies. Since ads that appeal to Japanese have a quality elusive to many Americans, better results will be achieved by Japanese professionals.

Advertising is not cheap. One ad in a high-circulation newspaper can cost as much as $8,000, depending on the day and the location of the ad. Adjuncts to image building, but ones not to be overlooked, are thoughtful, well-crafted brochures and business cards. These are invaluable and offer a comparatively inexpensive way to promote the institution. In any such public relations campaign there is a paramount consideration: the quality of the program must match the quality of the advertisements.

PARENTAL INVOLVEMENT

Much of the program's student recruitment success will depend on a carefully developed procedure for including parents in the recruitment efforts. One of the highest priorities of any Japanese family is to secure the best possible education for its children. Parents often begin saving for this even before a child is born. There are special prekindergarten schools, accelerated kindergartens, and grade schools that prepare students for the best private middle schools and high schools. These, in turn, are the schools that are noted for their ability to graduate students who can pass the entrance exams for one or more of the prestigious universities. Parallel to the public and private school system is the *juku* system—private, after-hours prep schools that specialize in university examination preparation. Obviously not every student in Japan is involved in the race for the limited number of openings at the handful of select universities. Thousands, however, do participate, and the dream of nearly every Japanese parent is to see his or her child graduate from a university.

Faced with this deeply rooted parental devotion and sacrifice, American programs need to convince the parents, and particularly the mother (Lebra 1976: 154), that the institution can and will provide the kind of education that will benefit their child. For many of the applicants, an American branch university may not be their first choice, and often they may not be the best students. If the scenario were completely reversed and an American family had the option of sending their child to Harvard or to a Japanese community college, where would the student go? It is not sufficient to simply convince the student. Although Japan is changing, the family unit and family values still remain intact. To compete, the American branch must offer the best possible program with a faculty of excellence and a long-term commitment. The investment of time, expense, and effort spent in the area of persuading the parents needs to be backed by the quality of the institution. This in turn will create a broad base of support for the institution and ensure its growth.

EDUCATION AND PHILOSOPHY

The consideration that respondents gave to the philosophical aspects of this enterprise was less than hoped for. Some showed a grasp and understanding of some of the problems facing the United States and Japan. Others indicated a lack of understanding that does not speak well for the role of leadership that is called for in a venture of this magnitude.

Traditionally, higher education in Japan has functioned as a selection process. By keeping the entrance quotas small through the use of examinations, they were able to build a reservoir of high talent for government and business. Universities in Japan are perceived in a hierarchical order. The university at the top of the pyramid is the most prestigious. Those on the lowest and widest base are the junior colleges. Job guarantees come with entrance to the universities on the most distinguished levels. Thus preserving the status quo, providing an atmosphere conducive to meeting other "right people," and maintaining an elitist element in society have become the goals of the university system.

American higher education goals have shifted since World War II. Prior to that war, the emphasis was on a liberal arts program designed to produce the "well-rounded person." The classics, from Aristotle to Shakespeare, and Latin, French, or German were an integral part of the curriculum. Today American higher education has moved toward a supply and demand process. An analogy can be drawn between supply-side economics and what might be termed supply-side education. In a supply-side economics, impediments to economic growth are believed to be disincentives to work and invest as a result of the level and structure of taxes. In education, admission standards and high levels of expectation were seen as impediments to growth. By lowering these standards, the universities became more accessible. The goals of American higher education have become blurred by attempting to meet the needs of a broader and broader spectrum of society.

Paradoxically, however, the basic difference between American higher education and Japanese higher education is that American higher education demands hard work and intense study, while Japanese higher education, on the other hand, is a place of rest and relaxation before facing the rigors of the workplace.

Some Differences Between Japanese And American Students

Americans tend to be aggressive and individualistic, while Japanese tend to be passive and group-oriented.

American students tend toward self-assuredness, while Japanese students tend to be self-effacing.

Japanese students tend to be more serious and respectful than American students.

Japanese students are more apt to follow directions than American students.

Japanese students have a larger capacity for study and memorization than American students.

Japanese students pay more attention to preparation and detail than American students.

American students tend to be critical and questioning, while Japanese students tend to accept the status quo or statements at face value.

OTHER TYPES OF PROGRAMS

Some alternative programs that are both innovative and non-traditional have been started in part because of the original plan proposed by Susumu Nikaido and House Majority Leader Gephardt. One example is The Japan Center for Michigan

Universities located in Hikone-shi, Shiga Prefecture. The program is designed to meet the needs of students who are majoring in many areas. The emphasis is on Japanese studies, but in a nontraditional manner. A variety of disciplines are joined together in a Japanese atmosphere where the language can be learned and acculturation is facilitated. There is an English language program for Japanese and a third component of short courses in a variety of disciplines. This approach is less rigid and affords the student a wide range of areas and ideas to explore.

There are other programs, such as The North Carolina Japan Center, that promote exchanges between Japan and the United States on a regular basis. They tend not to be locked into standard course offerings, but rather seek to share expertise on an expressed-need basis covering a broad spectrum of disciplines, science, business, and the arts.

THE OUTCOME

In many cases, the motivation for individual or institutional involvement on both sides of the Pacific has been money. In some cases, involvement has been based on personal aggrandizement and power. Despite the occasional wayward motivation, the survival of any of these projects depends primarily on the excellence of the programs. In setting up the first programs there has been much trial and error, both in planning and implementation. New programs, however, often continue to make the same mistakes as their predecessors. This is due to the lack of shared information. As a result, some of the programs will fail. The reason for specific failures are generally not disclosed, and this secrecy frustrates objective assessment of how the collapse might have been prevented.

One element the Japanese may have overlooked in the careful design and implementation of this undertaking is: do the Americans have the ability to transplant enough of the essence of American higher education to Japan to engender an atmosphere in which creativity and innovation can thrive? For the most part,

American educators are not aware that this is a goal. The primary motivation for many of the Japanese partners is not education or the stimulation of creativity. Thus programs in Japan depend on two things for their success: (1) the ability of the faculty to re-create the American classroom atmosphere, and (2) the number of non-Japanese students enrolled in the program. If 90 to 100 percent of the program is comprised of Japanese students, success is improbable. The very weight of the culture carried by the majority of the students will overshadow faculty efforts. On the other hand, since most of the programs are designed as transfer programs, the Americans, in seeking to increase enrollments at the home campus, may have inadvertently provided the key to success. By functioning basically as ESL funnels, the programs are sending the students to an effective language-development milieu rather than having to re-create it.

One thing is certain: regardless of the goals and motivation of the parties involved in this bold new venture, the machinery of a historic activity has been set in motion.

Chapter Eight

BUSINESS OPTIONS: AN OPEN DOOR

American business is still the primary force in the global economy. The fortunes of corporate America are inextricably tied to American education. If the one fails, so does the other, and American education is failing. American business has no choice except to get involved.

Corporate Japan has had the foresight to design and implement a plan to forge a link with American higher education as the path to creativity and innovation. Will corporate America continue to sit back and watch while America continues to undereducate those who will be responsible for its future?

AN OVERVIEW

Japanese business has traditionally been at the forefront of change in Japan. Merchants, artisans, and traders accompanied the embassies sent to China between A.D. 400 and 900. The knowledge, products, and skills that they brought back formed the basis for Japan's commercialism. The lack of raw materials contributed to the shaping of the attitude and thinking of Japan's merchant class. Survival and growth, even today, are still perceived as being synonymous with trade. Japanese businessmen who are in the vanguard with this attitude are quick to spot potential markets and opportunities.

In the 1980s the need to restructure the manufacturing sector forced itself upon Japan. The dilemma that arose was how to produce the type of individual who would meet the needs of corporate Japan without dismantling or placing undue strain on the existing higher education system. To challenge the educational establishment, which plays such an invaluable role in Japanese society, would be to deny the validity of the social structure of Japan. As a way to resolve the dilemma, Japan's businessmen formulated the radical educational strategy of importing American institutions of higher learning.

An example of a field in which Japan lacks skilled graduates, and an area targeted by the Ministry of International Trade and Industry (MITI) for priority development, is creative computer software. By the year 2000 the world market for software is expected to reach the $1 trillion mark. Currently, the United States controls about 70 percent of the $70–75 billion world market. As of now the Japanese are estimated to be four to five years behind in the ability to generate cutting-edge software programs. It pays to remember, however, that at one time the American auto-manufacturing industry also had a sizable lead over Japan in manufacturing technology. Fujitsu, Hitachi, and NEC, to name a few companies, are currently spending hundreds of millions of dollars on software research and development in order to catch up with the United States. Even though most of Japan's research in this area is product-led, this approach, too, can generate noteworthy progress.

The field of "fuzzy logic" provides a good example of the deep-rooted Japanese tradition of borrowing and adapting. Fuzzy logic has been around since the 1970s and has the capability to extend software logic beyond "on only" or "off only" functions. It was discarded by most American software designers as an anomaly. The Japanese, however, went on to harness this software capability as a control system for numerous appliances. One example of this is an air-conditioning unit that is able to sense if an individual enters or leaves the room. When this happens the unit's software program, which controls a sensor, makes the appropriate adjustment.

LANGUAGE AND CREATIVITY

Linguists generally make the case that language shapes the thought processes of the individual. One cannot answer a philosophical question about time in Japanese in the same manner in which one answers it in English. The concept behind the word *time* is different in both languages. The correlation between language and the culturally influenced processing of information should not be discounted in the educational process. This is not to suggest, however, that the development of English proficiency will necessarily lead to a mode of innovative and creative thinking, but rather that it manifestly does play an important role in how an individual can formulate and express thoughts. When Japanese students are asked what is the biggest difference they notice between the English and Japanese languages, they often reply that there is a greater "sense of freedom" in English.

There have been several occasions in recent Japanese history when English nearly became the official language of Japan. The notion was given serious consideration by the High Command of the Allied Occupation Task Force. The proposal was finally discarded, but not before lengthy debate among many Japanese scholars, businessmen, and politicians who were in favor of such a move. They believed that adopting English as an official national language would allow Japan to function more easily and competitively with Western nations.

The most recent serious challenge to Japan's monolingualism arrived with the computer. As has been noted, the Japanese writing style is particularly cumbersome. In order to generate one Japanese character, a computer must use two bytes. To generate one letter of an alphabet requires only one byte. This was an obstacle of gigantic proportions. It held back development for precious years and cost millions of dollars to overcome.

Ironically, one of the contributors to the breakthrough was IBM Japan Ltd.

There are many reasons why English has become the second language of Japan, but the most important fact is that by acquiring English proficiency, the Japanese are opening the door to a style of logic and problem solving that is not native to the Japanese language. Among the many Japanese studying in the United States are computer engineers sent there by their companies. On campuses across the United States from UCLA to MIT, one finds Japanese students clustered in the computer labs. These students are not relying on translation to gain knowledge; they are learning in English. The establishment of American institutions of higher learning in Japan is accelerating this process.

EDUCATION: THE BUSINESS OF BUSINESS

Today it has often become necessary for American business to furnish much of the education previously delivered by the formal education system. American elementary and secondary education is failing American higher education and, consequently, corporate America. American business currently spends a reported $210 billion a year on in-house education. Approximately 1 percent of this amount is being spent to teach or improve basic skills in reading, writing, and math (Applebee, Langer, and Mullis 1987: 4).

A decline in American industrial productivity began to show up in studies by the early 1970s. The last year in which the United States had a favorable trade balance with Japan was 1975. The decline of American education parallels the decline of corporate America. Part of the problem in American education lies in its image. Education has a history of functioning in isolation and independence. Educators have been considered necessary, but probably unable to function in the "real world." More prestige has generally been accorded to the rugged individual with a sixth-grade education who became a self-made millionaire than to any Nobel laureate. The ivory tower image was one that separated the education system from mainstream economic enterprise. Part of American folklore is the caricature of the bumbling college graduate unable to tie his own shoes or perform the most mundane workday task.

Education, realizing that it was badly out of step with the rest of society, began to experiment with novel approaches. Heavy emphasis was placed on newly designed school buildings, on textbooks filled with large, glossy illustrations to accompany written text, on mechanical and electronic teaching devices, and on numerous misunderstood and misapplied methodologies such as bilingual education, whole-language instruction, and new math. Unfortunately, standardized test data show that the result has been a steady decline in student performance in the fundamentals of reading, writing, and math.

In the mid-1970s, a handful of educators began to point out that declining test scores were evidence of deeply troubling problems. In 1983, the damning white paper *A Nation at Risk* provided a blueprint that outlined the extent of the damage. Seven years later, the downtrend has not been reversed. The damage extends to today's university classrooms, where future teachers are being trained. They are being taught by professors who have come full-cycle through the system of ever-lowering expectations that has characterized the education system for the past fifteen to twenty years. As a general rule, teachers teach what they have been taught and how they have been taught.

By the first half of the 1970s, some businesses were beginning to be alarmed by the number of job applicants who could not fill out a job application. Some high school systems attempted to forestall this problem by offering classes on how to fill out job applications. This approach did little to improve reading and writing skills on a broader scale. Examples of another approach aimed at resolving the problem were the host of programs funded by the government to serve the educationally disadvantaged. Some showed limited or temporary success; most did not.

Early in the 1980s, some businesses began taking an active role as advocates of reform and even as providers of financial support in some communities. This effort continues today, but unfortunately, it is random and uncoordinated. Several books have been published by prominent business figures offering plans for revising the American education system. Many of these, such as *Winning the Brain Race*, by Xerox CEO David Kearns, offer sound advice. The problem that remains is the lack of united effort or agreement inside or outside the educational community. Consequently, the problems proliferate and deepen. This is, unfortunately, happening at a time when the nature of the competition for global leadership and control demands the very best and brightest of players.

In the area of pure basic research, the American university system is the acknowledged leader. The system provides the time, atmosphere, and encouragement for researchers to explore new and untried areas. This notwithstanding, three factors that could potentially cripple this leadership are looming on the horizon.

First, one in four American students will not graduate from high school. Illiteracy and the more insidious functional illiteracy are increasing on a yearly basis. This places an ever-growing strain on the national economy by skewing the tax base disproportionately. Nonproductive citizens require more social services: housing subsidies, welfare, law enforcement, and child support, to name a few. As the United States becomes an aging society, these services must be supported by a decreasing number of taxpayers. Consequently, corporate America will be expected to shoulder a larger share of the burden. Faced with a shrinking labor pool, and one characterized by new employees with lower entry-level skills, business will find it increasingly difficult to compete in the global market.

The second negative factor is a shift in the demographics of the school-age population. The baby boom is over. The baby-boomers, many of whom today are well educated and affluent, are having fewer children. It is the lower socioeconomic stratum of the United States that has the highest birthrate and is the fastest growing segment of American society. The number of "at risk" children, those who are the least likely to complete high school, thus increases proportionately. As the process comes full-cycle, the number of potential well-educated employees and college students decreases, placing increasing strain on already overextended and mismanaged resources.

The third adverse factor is the shrinking teacher pool. Fewer and fewer of those who graduate from universities each year choose teaching as a career. By perceiving the teaching profession as a secondary occupation, American society is squandering its inheritance. By means of financial incentives and prestigious placements, society encourages those graduates who have the potential for excellence to enter corporate America. This loss to the teaching profession is not being replaced. True, there are and will always be good teachers. Salaries have gone up. Expenditure per pupil has increased. Student/teacher ratios have improved. Unfortunately, the prestige of the teaching profession has not increased and future prospects are not encouraging. Where will good teachers come from?

BUSINESS WITH JAPAN THROUGH AMERICAN EDUCATION

As part of the current educational experiment, Japan proposes to create an internship system whereby American students who graduate from the branch programs in Japan would be able to work for local Japanese firms. This would provide an ideal learning experience. Most mainland American institutions, however, have low expectations that their students will participate in these programs, and, consequently, the proposal may come to naught. There are a number of reasons for this, but lack of perceived incentives and the high cost of living in Japan are the two main deterrents.

Nonetheless, there is still a way for corporate America to make the difference and, at the same time, begin to create a realistic and positive program for doing business with the Japanese. Since the 1970s American business has been charging Japan with unfair trade practices. In many cases, the allegations have been true. On the other hand, too often the allegations have served as an excuse for not adapting or improving business practices. At times, as in the automobile industry, the higher quality of Japanese imports was challenged by advertising slogans rather than real product improvement.

There are, of course, American success stories in Japan. Some businessmen have been successful because they learned how things are done in Japan. They are aware of the great amount of attention that the Japanese pay to detail and the long-range planning that is now paying handsome dividends for the Japanese. Americans often scoff at the need to wear a tie and a three-piece suit—with the tie tight, the vest buttoned, and the coat on—in order to do business. In Japan, a business meeting is serious and the thinking is that no one can be serious with shirtsleeves rolled up and tie loosened. That is the after-work look. Japanese etiquette is subtle but demanding. Initial greetings, exchanging *meishi* (business cards), showing deference, understanding seating arrangements, following the speaking order, and taking leave, all are governed by precise norms of behavior. If a businessman does not adapt to these norms, he will offend his hosts and lessen chances for a successful business agreement. What is worse is that Americans often do not realize that they have been offensive, much less why. The establishment of American college and university programs in Japan provides corporate America with a golden opportunity to accrue information and develop capabilities previously available only to those companies with branches in Japan.

MEETING THE CHANGING NEEDS

The United States and particularly the community of commerce need individuals who read, write, and speak Japanese, as well as individuals able to understand Japanese businessmen and business practices. This educational experiment is a vehicle ideally suited to accomplish exactly that and at an affordable price. Sponsorship of students and scholarships can be tax-deductible. In exchange for maintaining a student for one to three years of study in Japan, an agreement would be negotiated whereby the graduate upon completion of his sojourn in Japan would work for the sponsor for an agreed-upon period of time at a competitive salary.

Students to be sponsored would be selected on the basis of mutual benefit, interest, and area of study. Options thus become broad-based rather than limited to majors in Asian studies. Insurance companies, advertising agencies, manufacturing of all types, law firms, and banking, to name just a few, have an opportunity to customize the education program to their specific needs. Participation is limited only by the needs of the business. Graduates of these programs become a source of new clients and new ideas. They become the crucial link for communicating with the Japanese mind, which is the force driving Japanese business.

The inverse side of the program is offering internships to participating Japanese students who will be coming to the United States to finish their degree. Many of these students would welcome an opportunity to combine study with on-the-job experience. In some cases, it would be feasible to establish a program in conjunction with a university, which would enable the student to obtain college credit for these internships. Working students would provide direct contacts with kindred businesses in Japan. As these students return to Japan, they become the basis for a whole new type of business interchange, one based on trust, personal affinity, and a common body of knowledge.

Whether or not Japan and the United States are going to be business partners is not the question. This is a fact that has already occurred. The question is: what kind of a partnership will it be? This newest educational venture provides the opportunity to shape and mold the nature of that partnership. It is a venture that does not require negotiating on trade barriers or changing any laws. It simply calls for the foresight to establish an active, long-range personnel plan based on company needs between now and the year 2000. Corporate America needs not only productive, literate, creative employees; it also needs personnel skilled in foreign diplomacy, customs, and languages. A good place to start is with American education in Japan.

Chapter Nine

SOME CONCLUSIONS

This newest Japanese venture has not been well received in the United States primarily because it has not been portrayed positively. The secrecy surrounding the activities by the educational institutions involved has not promoted a "good press." Japan bashing has created a negative atmosphere and has thus biased the general public about "things Japanese." Some American educators and politicians have seen this venture as a "brain drain" and want it stopped. The American public has been very poorly educated concerning the benefits of these programs. In fact, there seems to be an unspoken agreement to keep involvement as low-key as possible.

Politicians who in the beginning enthusiastically supported the concept have since done an about-face or become very silent about their involvement. Perhaps it is because Japan has become a scapegoat for many of the economic woes of the United States. In a recent article titled "Fear and Loathing of Japan," the observation was made that:

In some precincts a whiff of McCarthyism is in the air. Self-appointed watchdogs compile lists of academics and lobbyists who take Japanese money, as though the recipients were collaborating with an enemy power. A dozen Congressmen, including House Majority Leader Richard Gephardt, sent a letter to President Bush complaining that a consultant to his Council of Economic Advisers, University of Michigan economist Gary Saxonhouse, has also advised a research institute funded by Japan's Ministry of International Trade and Industry. (Smith 1990: 50)

Perhaps this explains what is happening and why there is no publicity about the program. Japan bashing is in. If, however, the administrators, educators, and consortia involved in this educational project truly believe that it is a beneficial and worthwhile endeavor, then it is their duty to expound the relevance and the advantages of this undertaking. Even though the Japanese are "picking up the tab" for the cost, American tax dollars and expertise are involved. The concept is definitely in need of a champion to provide the American public with some balanced media coverage.

CAN THE PROGRAM BE STOPPED?

Of all the American politicians and educators involved in this endeavor, few, if any, seem to have observed that at the root of all of this activity is Japan's awareness of her vulnerability and the need to overcome this by becoming self-sufficient. If Japan can borrow and adapt the means to create technology, she will have accomplished something that has never been done before. Will the United States join with Japan and make this an open, wholehearted joint venture? Improbable. there are some factions in the United States, both in politics and in education, that do not see this as a positive undertaking. There is an underlying aversion to learning from Japan. Will the project in any case continue? Yes, because Japan has the money to pay. This comes at a time when the United States is suffering severe financial difficulties, and in the next decade education and other social programs will be hard pressed to meet their commitments. Some institutions of higher learning will see the need to continue to be involved in projects such as this as part of their ability to survive financially.

GLOBAL RAMIFICATIONS

The advantages to be derived from any program of this nature are sure to include an awakening of intellectual curiosity and the perception that knowledge is useful. The program will provide the basis for an increased proficiency in English and Japanese and the acquisition of relevant skills applicable to business as well as academia. The world need for international skills and understanding is accelerating much faster than the ability to foster such expertise. World business markets are changing as rapidly as the world political scene. A united Germany, the European common market, a changing Eastern Europe, the rapid growth of the newly industrializing countries, all are indicators of what is to come in the next decade. Japan is looking ahead and has devised a plan to provide the kinds of personnel needed to cope with these new realities. The United States has the opportunity. Whether or not the opportunity will be seized is a question yet to be answered.

Appendix A

ONGOING STRUCTURAL CHANGES IN JAPANESE INDUSTRIES AND CORPORATIONS

Industries	Inducements	Moves in industries	Diversifications moves and tie-ups	Internationalizations
Primary industry				
Agriculture	· Increased import pressure as a result of expanded price gaps between domestic and foreign products · Varied demand for foods	· Improvement of domestic productivity · Product differentiation, production of a variety of products in a small lots	· Tourist farms · Food processing to add high value to products	· Efforts to increase exports by attending world trade fairs
Forestry	· Increased import as a result of the yen's appreciation and tariffs · Slow demand for domestic lumber and price declines	· Rationalization by cooperation and automation	· Revitalization of the forestry industry using forests for such purposes as camping sites · Practical development of new uses for lumber	
Fisheries	· Sharp fishing quota cuts and other intensified regulations imposed by foreign countries in overseas fishing grounds · Increased import as a result of active production and export by foreign countries, and stronger yen	· Shift to resource management-oriented fishing · Improvement of distribution and processing systems to provide highly value-added products, making the best use of inshore resources	· Expansion of trading activities, incl. export and import, of the larger firms	
Secondary industry				
Coal mining	· Expanded price gaps between domestic and foreign coal	· Reduction of capacity and integration of production · Implementation of cost-cutting measures, such as an introduction of automatic machinery and personnel cutback		
Foodstuff	· Slow demand growth, and increased demand for variety and higher quality	· Entry into the dine-out business and other related services	· Diversification into the biotechnology field	· Increased overseas production to cope with matured domestic food markets and expensive domestic agricultural products

Industry				
Textiles	· Increased demand for more fashionable and casual wear · Decreased competitiveness abroad because of the yen's appreciation and a gap in personnel costs	· Entry into related service business, in which highly value-added production and product differentiation are possible	· Reinforcement to make the machinery and synthetic resin sections less dependent on textiles	· Entry of service-related section into overseas market
Pulp/paper	· Decreased demand for industrial-use paper, and increased demand for information equipment-use paper · Decreased competitiveness abroad as a result of the yen's appreciation	· New commodity development to find new markets	· Diversification into the biotechnology field	· Increased offshore production to cut costs and boost overseas marketing activities
Chemicals	· Users industries' shift to overseas production	· Product differentiation and speciality production manufacturing · Cutback in excess capacity	· Diversification into the bio-technology and new material fields	· Increased offshore production to take advantage of cheaper raw materials and fuels and labor on the background of user industries' move to produce abroad
Petroleum	· Slow demand growth, progressive disparity in demand for oil · Liberalization of import in certain oil products	· Implementing excess capacity cutback · Upgrading equipment and facilities	· Multiple business management of gas stations · Some are trying to become general energy companies	
Cement	· Decreased competitiveness abroad as a result of the yen's appreciation	· Cutback in excess capacity, establishment of joint ventures to rationalize production and distribution systems	· Entry into the real estate business, and development of fine ceramics	
Iron & steel	· Sluggish domestic demand stemming from industrial structure's shift to tertiary industry and increased overseas production by user industries · Decreased competitiveness abroad as a result of the yen's appreciation	· Rationalization of production facilities and work force in iron and steel divisions	· Expansion of new material and electronics divisions	· Increased offshore production forced by import regulations of trade partner countries and also by user industries' move to produce abroad

Industries	Inducements	Moves in industries	Diversifications moves and tie-ups	Internationalizations
Aluminum smelting	· Loss of international competitiveness as a result of the yen's appreciation and increased energy costs	· Reduction of domestic output or withdrawal from production in Japan		· Increased overseas production to take advantage of cheaper materials and fuels abroad
Copper, lead, zinc processing	· User industries' shift to overseas production · Decreased competitiveness abroad as a result of the yen's appreciation		· Production of silicon and lead frames, and entry into high-tech fields, including new material development	· Increased overseas production to enter the advanced technology fields, and cooperation with foreign corporations
Home appliances	· Matured markets for TV sets and VTRs · Intensified trade frictions	· Development of new audiovisual and home automation products · Product differentiation by combining and systematizing various functions into one product	· Entry into information-related business, including the value-added network business	· Increased overseas production forced by intensified trade frictions · Horizontal division of labor with NICs
Electronics	· Increased demand for information-related equipment · Market expansion as a result of liberalization of telecommunication services · Intensified trade friction chiefly in the semiconductor field	· Reinforcement of comprehensive technology development power	· Reinforcement of software development divisions · Moves to become the general information and communication industry	· International technological cooperation and joint development · Increased offshore production forced by intensified trade friction
Shipbuilding, heavy machinery	· Decreased demand because of a slump in the shipping industry · Decreased competitiveness abroad as a result of the yen's appreciation	· Substantial cutback of equipment and personnel in shipbuilding divisions	· Expansion of the factory automation, aeronautics and space-related divisions · Research and development in the biotechnology and medical fields	· Joint aircraft development with U.S. firms
Automobiles	· Maturity of domestic markets and varied demand · Intensified trade friction, increasing presence of NICs	· Rationalization and product differentiation by introducing industrial robots and flexible manufacturing systems	· Diversification into the space and robot fields · Entry into the telecommunication business	· Reinforcement of overseas production systems through such measures as cooperation with foreign companies

Construction	· New construction demand created by the progress of information-oriented society · Strong foreign calls for Japan to open its construction markets	· Standardization of construction processes and materials · Introduction of robots into such processes as painting and flooring	· Expansion of construction, and moves to become engineering constructors · Cooperation with communications companies in relation to intelligent building construction	· Increased overseas activities to find new markets and also to cope with Japanese companies' stepped-up production and business activities abroad
Tertiary industry Power utilities	· Slow demand growth in volume, accompanied by structural changes	· Power resource development for stable supply of cheaper power	· Entry into the information and telecommunication business	
Distribution	· Varied demand, increased differences in demand of each person and shortening life of demand for one service · Progress in information management and distribution systems	· Introduction of point-of-sales and value-added network systems to establish efficient distribution systems	· Offering financial and information services · Business tie-ups with regional environment developers	· Opening of outlets abroad, and increased dealings in imported products
General trading	· Sluggish basic material industries, and the rise of the high technology-related industries · Decreased demand for financing by trading companies	· Introduction of office automation technology for efficient clerical work · Cutback of personnel in non-sales divisions	· Entry into such business fields as information, telecommunications, high-technology and services	· Increased triangular trading and counter purchasing · Establishment of financing subsidiaries abroad
Banks, securities brokerages	· Varied demand in fund procurement and management · Increased variety of financial products as a result of financial liberalization · Increase of foreign financial institutions in Japan	· Promotion of the third-round construction of the interbank on-line network to rationalize business further, and improvement of information management and analyzing systems	< Banks > · Reinforcement and expansion of the securities business · Business tie-up with securities and life insurance firms < Securities brokerages > · Offering of comprehensive financial services, including investment advisory service · Business tie-up with banks and life insurance firms	· Reinforcement and expansion of international divisions to enter overseas markets and also to boost the foreign exchange and securities business · Reinforcement and expansion of international divisions to cope with investment in foreign securities and active issuance of Euro-yen bonds

Industries	Inducements	Moves in industries	Diversifications moves and tie-ups	Internationalizations
Life insurance	· varied and specialized demand in the aging society	· Commodity development in the livelihood insurance field	· Business tie-up with banks	· Establishment of oversees subsidiary to invest in foreign securities and real estate
Real estate	· Increased demand for building as a result of the progress of office automation and an increase of foreign companies in Japan	· Enrichment of remodeling and consulting business	· Entry into the leasing, leisure and hotel business	· Active investment in overseas real estate
Leasing	· Progress of office automation and factory automation, an, equipment	· Development of new leasing	· Business tie-up with trust banks · Offering of comprehensive plant & equipment investment services	· Active international leasing services
Services for business companies (excl. leasing service)	· Rationalization at corporations, increased demand for information-related services · Increased demand for information processing services	< Information processing service > · Moves to become general information processing industry	· Promotion of the value-added network business in cooperation with firms in other business sectors	· Establishment of footholds abroad to promote software trading
Medical	· Aging of the society, an increase of nuclear families and women's advance to business fields	· Introduction of latest medical equipment	· Offering of new services related to medical care	· Offering of first-aid medical services abroad
Education	· Progress of the information-oriented society, and moves of internationalization · Emergence of a highly educated society, an increase of leisure time and a rise of varied and specialized demand	· Moves to cope with new demand, such as information processing techniques and the Japanese language · Opening new school courses · University extensions related to wordprocessors and personal computers · Special lectures at culture centers		· Increased international exchange of students and trainees · Repletion of foreign language education
Leisure, amusements, sports	· Repletion of physical needs, increased differences in demand of each person · Increase of overseas travels	· Development of unique concept theme parks	· Construction of multifunc-resort-lands equipped with sports facilities	· Import of software and game machines

Restaurants	· Increase of diners-out, increased demand for a variety of tastes	· Deployment of various kinds of outlets such as from 'family' restaurant to 'casual' restaurant	· Creation of multifunctional outlets in cooperation with firms in other business fields · Ventures to move abroad to join in growing overseas markets
Land transport	· Demand shift to automobiles and airplanes · Decreased physical distribution due to service orientation, and increased demand for sophisticated services	· Privatization of Japanese National Railway, and managerial rationalization · More sophisticated door-to-door delivery services	· Active diversification in business of the privatized Japanese National Railway · Launching of international door-to-door delivery services
Marine transport	· Worldwide surplus of bottoms, decreased competitiveness abroad as a result of the yen's appreciation, and decreased physical distribution due to service orientation	· Reduction of bottoms and personnel	· Moves to become the comprehensive distribution industry · Entry into the real estate business · Intermodal consistent transportation
Aerial transportation	· Increased demand for high-speed transport · Competition promoted by deregulation	· Stepped-up managerial rationalization following the scheduled privatization of Japan Air Lines	· Expansion of the hotel and travel agency business · Japanese governmental policy to allow more than two airline companies to engage in international flight services
Telecommunications	· Increased demand for intercorporation networks · Liberalization of telecommunication services	· Introduction of service differentiation strategy in response to active new entry from other business fields	· Operation of various kinds of value-added networks in tie-up with firms in other industries

Source: Economic Planning Agency 1988: Table II-3-1, 164–169.

Appendix B

AMERICAN COLLEGES AND UNIVERSITIES CURRENTLY INTERESTED IN THE JAPAN BRANCH PROGRAM

Presented by The International Lobby, Tokyo, November 1988

1. University of Alabama
2. Alabama A&M University
3. University of Alabama at Birmingham (SURA)
4. American University
5. Angelo State University (TIEC)
6. University of Arizona
7. Auburn University
8. Bemidji State University (SUSM)
9. Boston University
10. Brown University
11. University of California/Berkeley
12. University of California/Davis
13. University of California Extension
14. Catholic University
15. University of Central Florida
16. Central State University
17. Clark College
18. Clemson University (SURA)
19. University of Colorado at Boulder (MASUA)
20. Columbia University
21. Cornell University

22. University of Delaware (SURA)
23. Duke University
24. Eastern Oregon State College (OSSHE)
25. East Texas State University (TIEC)
26. Emory University
27. Fisk University
28. University of Florida
29. Florida A&M University
30. Florida Atlantic University
31. Florida Institute of Technology
32. Florida International University
33. Florida State University (SURA)
34. George Mason University
35. Georgetown University
36. George Washington University (SURA)
37. University of Georgia (SURA)
38. Georgia Institute of Technology
39. Hampton University
40. University of Hartford
41. University of Hawaii
42. Hollins College
43. University of Houston (TIEC)
44. Howard University
45. University of Idaho
46. University of Illinois
47. Illinois Institute of Technology
48. Iowa State University
49. James Madison University
50. John F. Kennedy University
51. Johns Hopkins University
52. University of Kansas (MASUA)
53. Kansas State University (MASUA)

54. University of Kentucky (SURA)
55. Lamar University (TIEC)
56. Lansing Community College
57. Laredo State University (TIEC)
58. Lincoln University
59. Louisiana State University (SURA)
60. Mankato State University (SUSM)
61. University of Maryland (SURA)
62. University of Massachusetts
63. Metropolitan State University (SUSM)
64. University of Miami
65. Michigan State University
66. Midwestern State University (TIEC)
67. Mississippi State University
68. University of Missouri/Columbia (MASUA)
69. University of Missouri/Kansas City (MASUA)
70. University of Missouri/Rolla (MASUA)
71. University of Missouri/St. Louis (MASUA)
72. University of Montana
73. Moorhead State University (SUSM)
74. Morehouse College
75. Morgan State University
76. University of Nebraska at Lincoln (MASUA)
77. University of Nebraska at Omaha (MASUA)
78. University of New Mexico
79. University of New York State at Binghamton
80. Norfolk State University
81. North Carolina A&T State University
82. University of North Carolina at Chapel Hill (SURA)
83. North Carolina State University (SURA)
84. University of North Florida
85. Northrop University

86. North Texas State University (TIEC)
87. Northwestern University
88. Ohio University
89. University of Oklahoma (MASUA)
90. Oklahoma State University (MASUA)
91. Old Dominion University
92. University of Oregon (OSSHE)
93. Oregon Health Sciences University (OSSHE)
94. Oregon Institute of Technology (OSSHE)
95. Oregon State University (OSSHE)
96. University of Pennsylvania
97. University of Permian Basin
98. Portland State University (OSSHE)
99. University of Puget Sound
100. University of Richmond
101. Saginaw Valley State College
102. Sam Houston State University
103. San Angelo State University
104. Santa Monica College
105. Seton Hall University
106. University of South Carolina
107. University of Southern California
108. University of Southern Florida
109. Southern Illinois University at Carbondale (MASUA)
110. Southern Oregon State College (OSSHE)
111. South Texas State University
112. Southwest State University (SUSM)
113. Southwest Texas State (TIEC)
114. St. Cloud State University (SUSM)
115. St. John's University
116. St. Louis University
117. Sul Ross State University (TIEC)

118. Temple University
119. University of Tennessee at Chattanooga
120. Tennessee State University
121. Texas A&I University (TIEC)
122. Texas A&M University (TIEC)
123. University of Texas at Arlington (TIEC)
124. University of Texas at Austin (TIEC)
125. University of Texas at Dallas
126. University of Texas at El Paso (TIEC)
127. University of Texas at Permian
128. University of Texas at Tyler (TIEC)
129. University of Texas Health Science Center, San Antonio
130. Texas Southern University (TIEC)
131. Texas Tech University (TIEC)
132. Tufts University
133. Tulane University
134. University of Utah
135. University of Virginia
136. Virginia Commonwealth University
137. Virginia Polytechnic Institute & State University
138. Virginia State University
139. Wake Forest University
140. Washington University
141. Western Oregon State College (OSSHE)
142. Western Texas College
143. University of West Florida
144. West Texas State University (TIEC)
145. West Virginia University (SURA)
146. Wilberforce University
147. College of William & Mary
148. Winona State University (SUSM)
149. University of Wisconsin/Madison

150. University of Wisconsin/Milwaukee
151. Yale University

CONSORTIUM ASSOCIATIONS, WITH NUMBER OF MEMBER SCHOOLS

ASCG (Asia Studies Consortium of Georgia)	33
MASUA (Mid-America State Universities Association)	9
OSSHE (Oregon State System of Higher Education)	8
SURA (Southwestern Universities Research Association	35
SUSF (State University System of Florida)	9
SUSM (State University System of Minnesota)	7
TIEC (Texas International Education Consortium)	20

Appendix C

DRAFT PROPOSED GUIDELINES FOR THE EVALUATION OF BRANCH CAMPUSES OF UNITED STATES UNIVERSITIES IN JAPAN

Presented by the U.S. Foundation for International Economic Policy, November 28, 1989

AUTHORIZATION

1. The U.S. institution documents the accepted legal basis for its operations in the host country.

2. The international program has received all appropriate internal approvals, and/or that of the governing board.

3. The U.S. institution, or institution within a group, system, consortium or regional association, with a branch campus program, has received accreditation from a regional accrediting body recognized by the Council on Post-Secondary Accreditation and/or the U.S. Department of Education. Participating institutions have approval to include the branch campus within its accredited status and will seek an on-site accreditation visit within a reasonable amount of time. (TO BE DISCUSSED: The institution will include these guidelines within the goal statement against which the accrediting agency will compare the performance of the institution.)

SCOPE AND RESOURCES

4. The institution providing a branch campus program is at the baccalaureate level or higher.

5. The institution currently uses and assures the continuing use of adequate physical facilities for its international educational program, including classrooms, offices, libraries and laboratories.

6. Upon request, the U.S. institution provides evidence of financial soundness and stability.

7. English is the primary language of instruction at the Japanese branch.

JAPANESE AND U.S. STUDENTS

8. Students recruited for the Japan campus will be selected in accordance with criteria similar to those used to select students for the U.S. campus. Students not from the United States will be evaluated with an awareness for the cultural difference between students from their native country and the expectations of the U.S. university.

9. The U.S. institution has a clear written agreement in which it establishes plans for protecting the academic credits of students who have not completed a pre-determined educational objective if and when the U.S. institution terminates its branch campus.

10. The U.S. university has established goals for participation by U.S. students in the branch campus program.

11. The U.S. university has established and distributed guidelines for the evaluation of the English as a Second Language (ESL) program.

12. All academic credits earned in Japan are recorded within the official records of the U.S. campus as transferable credit for the students concerns, and all academic credits are applicable to degree programs.

CONTROL AND ADMINISTRATION

13. The Japanese branch campus program is governed by a written agreement, in English, between the institutions involved.

14. The U.S. university system, consortium or association has designated a single administrative unit responsible for administration and U.S.-based operation of the Japan branch campus.

15. The U.S. university controls the academic program, including curriculum, course offerings and academic organization and administration.

16. The U.S. university controls all faculty qualification and selection, including whether the faculty be U.S. or local hire.

17. The U.S. university controls all funds designated for the delivery of academic programs, including costs for administration, faculty and staff, and classroom facilities. The budget has been estab-

lished as a determined amount, based on either a lump sum or a fixed tuition for individual enrollees.

ETHICS AND PUBLIC DISCLOSURE

18. The U.S. university has not sold or franchised the rights to its name in Japan in return for a lump sum, annual payment or management fee, whether expressed in terms of a fixed amount or a percentage of income collected by the Japanese entity.

19. The U.S. university, and its Japanese partner, promote the branch campus program with factual, fair and accurate public communication about the goals, objectives, academic programs, degree studies and student services which are to be found on the branch campus. Such information will be reviewed by appropriate administrative officials at the main administrative office in the United States and found to be true and correct.

Appendix D

A PROPOSAL TO ESTABLISH AMERICAN UNIVERSITIES IN JAPAN

Presented by
The U.S.A.-Japan Committee for Promoting Trade Expansion

When American universities are established in Japan, the following is expected of them:

(1) The universities are regarded as the Japanese branch of the American main campus.

(2) University management guarantees that the university is both an academically and economically sound operating institution.

(3) Educational policy is exactly the same at the Japanese campus as at the main American campus.

Through the establishment of such universities the following benefits will be expected in Japan:

(1) Universities are to become a base of international culture for the youth of various nationalities and a place where students have access to American education while residing in Japan.

(2) Through the participation of many nationalities with their varied and specific historical, political, and cultural backgrounds, these proposed colleges and universities will play a significant role in the enhancement of international understanding.

(3) Foreign students, particularly from Asian nations, can attain the same education as students in America.

(4) By introducing a new phase into Japanese education, the universities will become a cornerstone to build a "learning-oriented society" instead of a "school-carrier society."

(5) The establishment of this type of community could serve for the development of a more coherent and mutually binding relationship between the academic institution and its surrounding community.

(6) The function of this type of academic institution could contribute to the reduction of trade friction through the enhancement of international understanding.

The universities should have the following characteristics:

(1) The system of the universities is to be established according to the American educational system.

(2) The admission to the universities will be based on the same procedure as in the United States.

(3) The universities are to be open to any qualified person regardless of race or nationality.

(4) The proposed academic institution is to be for the higher education of students in all academic areas.

(5) All lectures are to be given in English.

(6) The lectures in some specialized courses will be financed by Japanese private firms, under a donor system. For instance, course "X" may be sponsored by company "Y" with the company undertaking all financial responsibility.

(7) The fellowships and scholarships are to be provided by Japanese industrial and business groups.

(8) The universities are considered as a part of an integrated community. Thus, students are provided the opportunity of staying either in university dormitories or with Japanese families.

The committee to establish American universities in Japan is being formed. The following have been determined.

The proposed sites . . . are to be in several locations throughout Japan, with incentive measures being introduced to make the universities economically operative. Such measures include the following:

(a) Public land will be made available either free of charge or at a reduced price or under a lease program.

(b) The construction of the campus and the related facilities may be undertaken by Japan side and it will be released out to American colleges and universities under a long term condition.

(c) The endowment of chair will be underwritten by Japanese business group, and other financial assistances such as scholarships, etc. may be arranged.

(d) Host family arrangement for foreign students will be provided by the host communities.

(e) Integrated academic exchange and collaboration with local higher institutes are provided in order to enhance the challenging academic environment.

(f) Internship system will be provided, whereby upon graduation students may be able to work for Japanese local firms.

The benefits of the American—Japanese university connection include:

(1) Public benefits such as:

(a) Educating students to enable them to become internationally aware and competent in understanding various cultures.

(b) Deepening mutual understanding through the promotion of international fellowships, thus contributing to the reduction of friction not only between America and Japan (relative to the current trade friction) but among all nations.

(c) Aiming at an international education system, with the fundamental philosophy being focused on the opening of Japanese educational market.

(2) The creation of an integrated academic community.

(a) Effective utilization of public holding land through the program of utilization of private sector resources.

(b) Emphasis to be placed on an integrated academic community. It is designed to create cooperative entities, making the university a part of the surrounding community.

Appendix E

INTERNATIONAL LOBBY FOR THE ENHANCED EQUILIBRIUM OF TRADE AND ECONOMY

■ The Japanese Members of the Committee

Honorary Chairman, Susumu Nikaido
Member of the House of Representatives (L.D.P)
Former Vice-President of the L.D.P
Senior Advisor of the L.D.P

Honorary Vice-Chairman, Masumi Esaki
Member of the House of Representatives (L.D.P)
Former Minister of International Trade & Industry
Chairman, Special Committee for International
Economic Measures of the L.D.P
Policy Research Council

Honorary Vice-Chairman, Tadashi Kuranari
Member of the House of Representatives (L.D.P)
Former Minister of Foreign Affairs
President, Japan-EC Parliamentarians' Friendship
League

Honorary Vice-Chairman, Mutsuki Kato
Member of the House of Representatives (L.D.P)
Former Minister of Agriculture, Forestry & Fisheries
Chairman, Research Commission on Economics and
Commodity Prices of the L.D.P Policy Research
Council

Honorary Vice-Chairman, Iichiro Hatoyama
Member of the House of Councillors (L.D.P)
Former Minister of Foreign Affairs
Deputy Chairman, Special Committee for
International Economic Measures of the L.D.P Policy
Research Council

Chairman, Yoshiro Hayashi
Member of the House of Representatives (L.D.P)
Former Minister of Health and Welfare
Deputy Chairman, Special Committee for
International Economic Measures of the L.D.P Policy
Research Council

Member, Tsutomu Hata
Member of the House of Representatives (L.D.P)
Former Minister of Agriculture, Forestry & Fisheries
Chairman, Commission on Agricultural Policy of the
L.D.P Policy Research Council

Member, Kazuo Aichi
Member of the House of Representatives (L.D.P)
Chairman, Standing Committee on Education
Director General, L.D.P Research Bureau

Member, Motoo Shiina
Member of the House of Representatives (L.D.P)
Whip, Special Committee on Security (H.R.)
Deputy Chairman, L.D.P Policy Research Council

Member, Kohji Kakizawa
Member of the House of Representatives (L.D.P)
Former Parliamentary Vice-Minister of Transport
Deputy-Director General, L.D.P International
Bureau

■ The American Members of the Committee

Chairman, Richard A. Gephardt
Representative, (Democrat) MO
Sponsor of Trade Emergency and Export
Promotion Act
Ways and Means Committee Trade Sub-committee

Member, Max Baucus
Senator, (Democrat) MT
Small Busines Committee,
Finance Committee, International Trade Sub-Com.

Member, Wendell H. Ford
Senator, (Democrat) KY
Commerce, Science, and Transportation Committee

Member, Albert Gore, Jr.
Senator, (Democrat) TN
Commerce, Science, and Transportation Committee

Member, John F. Kerry
Senator, (Democrat) MA
Foreign Relations Com., International Economic
Policy Sub-com., East Asian & Pacific Affairs
Sub-Committee

Member, George J. Mitchell
Senator, (Democrat) ME
Finance Committee, International Trade
Sub-Committee

Member, Les AuCoin
Representative, (Democrat) OR
Appropriations Committee

Member, Donald L. Bonker
Representative, (Democrat) WA
Foreign Affairs Committee, Chairman of
International Economic Policy and Trade
Sub-Committee

Member, Julian C. Dixon
Representative, (Democrat) CA
Appropriations Committee

Member, John J. Duncan
Representative, (Democrat) TN
Secretary of Ways and Means Com.

Member, Richard J. Durbin
Representative, (Democrat) IL
Budget Committee

Member, Thomas S. Foley
Representative, (Democrat) WA
Majority Leader, Budget Committee

Member, Bill Frenzel
Representative, (Republican) MN
Secretary of House Administration Com.
Ways and Means Committee

Member, Sam M. Gibbons
Representative, (Democrat) FL
Ways and Means Committee
Chairman of Trade Sub-Committee

Member, Barbara B. Kennelly
Representative, (Democrat) CT
Ways and Means Committee

Member, Mickey Leland
Representative, (Democrat) TX
Energy and Commerce Committee

Member, Trent Lott
Representative, (Republican) MS
Minority Whip, Rules Committee

Member, Constance A. Morella
Representative, (Republican) MD
Science, Space & Technology Committee

Member, Robert T. Matsui
Representative, (Democrat) CA
Ways and Means Committee
Trade Sub-Committee

Member, Mary Rose Oakar
Representative, (Democrat) OH
Banking, Finance, and Urban Affairs Com.

Member, Dan Rostenkowski
Representative, (Democrat) IL
Chairman of Ways and Means Committee
Trade Sub-Committee

Member, Ike Skelton
Representative, (Democrat) MO
Small Business Com., Chairman of Export
Opportunities and Special Small Business Problems
Sub-Committee

Member, Jim Wright
Representative, (Democrat) TX
Speaker of the House, Budget Committee

■ Steering Committee Members

Saburo Ohkita, Ph.D
Adviser, Ministry of Foreign Affairs

Shoichi Akazawa
Chairman, JETRO

Naohiro Amaya
Former Councillor for the Ministry of
International Trade and Industry

Ichiro Yoshikuni
President, Japan Convention Center Co., Ltd.

Jiro Ushio
Chairman, Social Engineering Institute

Kaoru Shimofusa, Ph.D.
Emeritus Professor, Tokyo University

Chiyoji Misawa
Chairman, Misawa Homes Institute of
Research and Development

Appendix F

RESEARCH QUESTIONNAIRE

I. NATURE OF THE PROGRAM

Approval to implement the program comes from the: State Board [__], Legislature [__], Board of Regents [__], Faculty Senate [__], Other _____.

The program's accreditation will come from the _____ Regional Accreditation Association. If other type of accreditation, please describe _____.

The program will be a: Branch of the Main Campus [__], Self-Maintained Autonomous Unit [__], Joint-Venture (Japanese/U.S.) [__]. If other, please explain _____.

Administrative personnel will be : Americans from the Main Campus [__], Japanese [__], Japanese and American [__]. If other, please explain _____.

Type of Program

1. Primarily a Transfer Program (students transfer back to the main campus or other institution): Yes [__]   No [__]

2. Full degree-granting program: A.A. [__], B.A. [__], M.A. [__], Ph.D. [__].

3. Teaching English as a Second Language is a: Primary Component [__], Secondary Component [__], Not Important [__].

4. If other, please describe _____

Academic Year: Semester [__], Quarter [__], Trimester [__].

The program is intended primarily for: Japanese [__], Americans [__], Other Nationalities _____.

Anticipated number of students: First Year _____ , Second Year _____ , Third Year _____ .

Anticipated percent of students: Japanese _____ , American _____ , Other Nationalities _____ .

II. FISCAL

The primary source of funding will be the: Main Campus [__], Japanese Government [__], Prefecture [__], City [__], Private American Foundation _____ , Private Japanese Foundation _____ .
If other, please describe: _____ .

Anticipated start-up cost for the first year: $25,000-$50,000 [__], $50,000-$100,000 [__], $100,000-$200,000 [__], Other Amount _____ .

What percent of start-up funds have been allocated for the program? 0% [__], 100% [__], Other % _____ .

For what years has the budget been established? _____

The anticipated start-up date is: _____[month] _____[year].

III. LOGISTICS

What type of operating license will your program have from the Japanese Government?

_____

Where will your program be located? City _____ , Prefecture _____ .

Are the facilities (physical plant) in place? Yes [__] No [__]

The facilities must be: built [__], remodeled [__], leased [__]. If leased, number of years _____ , provided by the Japanese [__]. If other arrangement, please explain _____ .

How will instructors/staff be recruited? Main Campus Transfer [__], Recruited in Japan [__], Recruited in the U.S. [__], Other _____

Will the program provide housing for the staff?
_____

Does the program have an orientation program for staff? Yes [___] No [___] If Yes, please provide a copy or a summary.

IV. STUDENT RECRUITMENT

What methods will the program use to attract students: Newspaper [___], Television [___], Ad Agency [___]. Please include any recruitment brochures or plans.

Does the program have an orientation plan for the students? Yes [___] No [___]. If Yes, please include any brochures or plan summaries.

Does the program have an orientation program for the parents? Yes [___] No [___]. If Yes, please include this with your reply.

How important do you see parental involvement in student recruitment? Very important [___], Important [___], Minimally Important [___], Not important [___]

How will textbooks be acquired? From Japan [___], From the U.S. [___]. If other, please explain _____

Does the program have a committee for textbook selection? Yes [___] No [___]

Have criteria for textbook selection been established? Yes [___] No [___] If Yes, please include a summary of the criteria.

V. PHILOSOPHY

The purpose of these subjective questions is to get an overview of opinions so that they can be shared with others. Be as brief or as lengthy as your time and inclination permit.

1. What do you see as the goals of American higher education in comparison with the goals of Japanese higher education?

2. What do you see as the basic difference between American higher education and Japanese higher education?

3. What are some of the benefits that Japanese students can gain from your program?

4. What are some of the basic differences between American students and Japanese students?

BIBLIOGRAPHY

Applebee, Arthur N., Judith A. Langer, and Ina V. S. Mullis. *Learning to Be Literate in America*. Princeton, N.J.: National Assessment of Educational Progress, 1987.

Aston, W. G. *A History of Japanese Literature*. Tokyo: Charles E. Tuttle, 1972.

Boxer, C. R. *The Christian Century in Japan*. London: Cambridge University Press, 1951.

Braddon, Russell. *The Other Hundred Year War*. London: Collins, 1983.

Campbell, John Creighton, ed. *Parties, Candidates, and Voters in Japan: Six Quantitative Studies*. Ann Arbor: University of Michigan Press, 1981.

Chamberlain, Basil Hall. *Japanese Things: Being Notes on Varied Subjects Connected with Japan*. 5th ed., rev. Tokyo: Charles E. Tuttle, 1970. Original ed. 1905.

Christopher, Robert C. *Second to None*. Tokyo: Charles E. Tuttle, 1987.

Denison, Edward F., and William K. Chung. *How Japan's Economy Grew So Fast*. Washington, D.C.: Brookings Institution, 1976.

Duke, Benjamin. *The Japanese School*. New York: Praeger, 1986.

Duus, Peter. *The Rise of Modern Japan*. Boston: Houghton Mifflin, 1976.

Economic Planning Agency. *Japan in the Year 2000*. Tokyo: Japan Times, 1985.

_____. *Economic Survey of Japan 1986–1987*. Tokyo: Printing Bureau, Ministry of Finance, 1988.

_____. *Economic Survey of Japan 1989–1990*. Tokyo: Printing Bureau, Ministry of Finance, 1990.

"Emperor's Life in Retrospect." *Asahi Evening News* (Tokyo). January 7, 1989.

Fukami, Akiko. "Lifestyle 1." *Japan Times*. February 26, 1989.

Hall, Ivan Parker. *Mori Arinori*. Cambridge, Mass.: Harvard University Press, 1973.

Hall, John W. "The Nature of Traditional Society." In *Political Modernization in Japan and Turkey*, edited by Robert E. Ward and Dankwart A. Rustow. Princeton, N.J.: Princeton University Press, 1964.

Higashi, Chikara, and G. Peter Lauter. *The Internationalization of the Japanese Economy*. Boston: Kluwer, 1987.

Horio, Teruhisa. *Educational Thought and Ideology in Modern Japan*. Edited and translated by Steven Platzer. Tokyo: University of Tokyo Press, 1988.

Hyoe, Murakami, and Thomas J. Harper, eds. *Great Historical Figures of Japan*. Tokyo: Japan Culture Institute, 1978.

Ishii, Ryosuke. *A History of Political Institutions in Japan*. Tokyo: University of Tokyo Press, 1980.

Iwaki, Akinori. "Firms Scour U.S. Colleges for Japanese Graduates." *Japan Economic Journal*. March 1988.

Japan Economic Institute of America, ed. *Japan's Industrial Policies*. Washington, D.C.: Japan Economic Institute of America, 1984.

JETRO, ed. *NIPPON 1988*. Tokyo: Japan External Trade Organization, 1988.

Keizai Koho Center. *Japan 1986: An International Comparison*. Tokyo: Keizai Koho Center, 1986.

Kirr, Susan. "Japanese Universities Contemplate Reform." *Japan Times*. March 16, 1988.

Kitazume, Takashi. "Cities Want U.S. Universities to Boost Economies." *Japan Times*. February 25, 1987.

Lebra, Takie Sugiyama. *Japanese Patterns of Behavior*. Honolulu: University Press of Hawaii. 1976.

Lehman, Jean-Pierre. *The Roots of Modern Japan*. London: Macmillan, 1982.

Lincoln, Edward J. *Japan: Facing Economic Maturity*. Washington, D.C.: Brookings Institution, 1988.

Makino, Noboru. *Decline and Prosperity*. Tokyo: Kodansha International, 1987.

Miller, Roy Andrew. *The Japanese Language*. Chicago: University of Chicago Press, 1967.

_____. *Japanese and the Other Altaic Languages*. Chicago: University of Chicago Press, 1971.

_____. *The Japanese Language in Contemporary Japan: Some Sociolinguistic Observations*. AEI-Hoover Policy Studies, no. 22. Washington, D.C.: American Enterprise Institute for Public Policy Research, 1977.

Ministry of Foreign Affairs. *Information Bulletin 1986–1987*. Tokyo: Japan Times, 1987.

_____. *Information Bulletin 1988–1989*. Tokyo: Japan Times, 1989.

_____. *Information Bulletin 1989–1990*. Tokyo: Japan Times, 1990.

Mombusho. Ministry of Education, Science and Culture. Tokyo: Printing Bureau, Ministry of Finance, 1982.

Morris, William, ed. *The American Heritage Dictionary of the English Language*. New York: Houghton Mifflin, 1976.

Munro, Neil Gordon. *Prehistoric Japan*. Yokohama, 1911.

Nakamura, Takafusa, and Bernard R. G. Grace. *Economic Development of Modern Japan*. Tokyo: Ministry of Foreign Affairs, 1987.

Nippon Steel Human Resource Development Company. *Nippon: The Land and Its People*, Tokyo: Gakuseisha Publishing, 1988.

Nourse, Mary A. *Kodo: The Way of the Emperor*. New York: Bobbs-Merrill, 1940.

OERI Japan Study Team. *Japanese Education Today*. Washington, D.C.: U.S. Government Printing Office, 1987.

Palmer, Aaron Haight. *Origin of the Mission to Japan*. Washington, D.C.: Henry Polkinhorn Printer, 1857. Reprint, Wilmington: Scholarly Resources, 1973.

Passin, Herbert. *Society and Education in Japan*. Tokyo: Kodansha International, 1987.

Pearce, David W., ed. *Macmillan Dictionary of Modern Economics*. London: Macmillan, 1986.

Reischauer, Edwin O.. *Japan: Past and Present*, 3rd ed. Tokyo: Charles E. Tuttle, 1987.

Saddler, A. L. *A Short History of Japan*. Sydney: Angus and Robertson, 1962.

Sansom, George. *A History of Japan to 1334*. Reprint. Kent, England: 1978.

Smith, Lee. "Fear and Loathing of Japan." *Fortune*. February 26, 1990.

"Takeshita's Policy Speech." *Japan Times*. February 11, 1989.

Teikoku. *Complete Atlas of Japan*, 9th ed. Tokyo: Teikoku-Shoin, 1987.

Todd, Cynthia. "Area Universities Joining Japanese Project." *St. Louis Post-Dispatch*, July 7, 1987.

Tsunoda, Ryusaku, et al. *Sources of Japanese Tradition*. New York: Columbia University Press, 1958.

Vance, Timothy J. *An Introduction to Japanese Phonology*. Albany: State University of N.Y. Press, 1987.

Watanuki, Joji. *Politics in Postwar Japanese Society*. Tokyo: University of Tokyo Press, 1977.

White, Merry. *The Japanese Educational Challenge*. Tokyo: Kodansha International, 1988.

Woronoff, Jon. *The Japan Syndrome.* New Brunswick, N.J.: Transaction Books, 1986.

_____. *Asia's "Miracle" Economies.* Armonk, N.Y.: M. E. Sharp, 1987.

Wray, Harry, and Hilary Conroy, eds. *Japan Examined.* Honolulu: University of Hawaii Press, 1983.

Zimmerman, Mark. *How to Do Business with the Japanese.* Tokyo: Charles E. Tuttle, 1987.

INDEX

ABOUT THE AUTHOR

NICHOLAS J. HAIDUCEK is currently an Education Advisor to a major corporation in Tokyo and was formerly Director of Education at Tokyo American College in Japan. He has taught and developed language programs in many parts of the world, including Japan, Mexico, Central America, Alaska, and Spain.
Dr. Haiducek holds a Ph.D. in Education with emphasis in Applied Linguistics and Second Language Methodology from the University of New Mexico and an M.A. in English from Emporia State University, Emporia, Kansas.